ISAAC SINGER
THE FIRST CAPITALIST

ALEX I ASKAROFF

COUNTRY BOOKS

Published by Country Books/Ashridge Press
Courtyard Cottage, Little Longstone, Bakewell, Derbyshire DE45 1NN
Tel: 01629 640670
e-mail: dickrichardson@country-books.co.uk
www.countrybooks.biz
www.sussexbooks.co.uk

ISBN 978-1-910489-05-5 (paperback)
First Edition
ISBN 978-1-910489-07-9 (hardback)
First Edition

© 2014 Alex I. Askaroff

The rights of Alex I. Askaroff as author of this work have
been asserted by him in accordance with the
Copyright, Designs and Patents Act 1993.

All rights reserved. No part of this publication may be reproduced,
stored in a retrieval system, or transmitted, in any way or form, or by
any means, electronic, mechanical, photocopying, or otherwise,
without the prior permission of the author and publisher.

British Library Cataloguing in Publication Data.
A catalogue record for this book is available from the British Library.

BISAC Subject Headings: Biographical
CIP Library Reference: Biographical

Printed and bound in England by:
4edge Ltd, Hockley Essex. Tel: 01702 200243

Dedication

To my family and friends who are always in my thoughts.

Acknowledgement

Cover design by Tom Askaroff. I must thank Corrinne Askaroff for her help. Corrinne tirelessly improves my often messy work, thank you, thank you, thank you. Also to Dick Richardson of Country Books who takes on my work with so much enthusiasm.

Every effort has been taken to ascertain that the images reproduced here are by permission, owned by Alex Askaroff, Sewalot.com or are in the public domain. If any copyright holder believes that this is not the case Country Books would be pleased to be informed.

Contents

Introduction: My Obsession	11
Chapter 1 Isaac Merritt Singer: His Roots	20
Chapter 2 *Give me your tired, your poor, your huddled masses yearning to breathe free* Isabelle Eugenie Boyer Part 1	22
Chapter 3 The Beginning of A Legend	27
Chapter 4 1823	30
Chapter 5 Isaac's First Wife: Catherine Maria Haley	33
Chapter 6 The Baltimore Strolling Players	35
Chapter 7 The Merritt Players	38
Chapter 8 1843	41
Chapter 9	43
Chapter 10 George B Zieber	46
Chapter 11 Orson C Phelps	48
Chapter 12 The Famous Bet	52

CHAPTER 13 HISTORY IS MADE	56
CHAPTER 14	61
CHAPTER 15	65
CHAPTER 16	68
CHAPTER 17 THE CUNNING ISAAC & EDWARD CLARK	70
CHAPTER 18 ZIEBER IS REMOVED	75
CHAPTER 19	79
CHAPTER 20 HOWE BEATS SINGER IN COURT!	82
CHAPTER 21 FIGHT, FIGHT…	91
CHAPTER 22 GEORGE ROSS MCKENZIE 1820-1892	93
CHAPTER 23	95
CHAPTER 24 THE FIRST HIRE PURCHASE SCHEME	97
CHAPTER 25 1857	101
CHAPTER 26	104
CHAPTER 27 MASS PRODUCTION	107
CHAPTER 28	111
CHAPTER 29 1859	114
CHAPTER 30	116
CHAPTER 31 1860	118
CHAPTER 32	122
CHAPTER 33 ISAAC'S ARREST	123

Chapter 34	129
Chapter 35	132
Chapter 36 Isabelle Eugenie Boyer: Part 2	137
Chapter 37 1863	140
Chapter 38 The Singer Manufacturing Company	142
Chapter 39 The Castle	145
Chapter 40	149
Chapter 41 Isaac Prepares to Leave America	155
Chapter 42	157
Chapter 43 Franco-Prussian War	159
Chapter 44	161
Chapter 45 The Wigwam Begins	164
Chapter 46	167
Chapter 47	170
Chapter 48 Birthday Celebrations at Oldway	174
Chapter 49 Alice's Wedding	179
Chapter 50 Death of a Pioneer	183
Chapter 51 The King is Dead, Long Live the King Isaac's Will	188
Chapter 52	194
Chapter 53	196

CHAPTER 54 ISABELLE EUGENIE BOYER PART 3
  VICOMTESSE D'E ESTENBURGH   199

CHAPTER 55 OLDWAY   204

CHAPTER 56 ISAAC SINGER'S WOMEN AND KNOWN CHILDREN 207

CHAPTER 57   212

CHAPTER 58 PARIS EUGENE SINGER   217

CHAPTER 59 PARIS SINGER & PALM BEACH   224

CHAPTER 60   227

CHAPTER 61 FRANKLIN MORSE SINGER & FLORENCE SINGER 229

CHAPTER 62 THE FINAL CHAPTER   232

AND FINALLY A BIG THANK YOU   235

INTRODUCTION

My Obsession

What a man! As a child growing up in the sewing industry, I was enthralled to hear stories of Isaac Singer. He had lived the American dream; a true 'rags to riches' story that all went wrong. But in a final twist, somewhere between wars and wives Isaac Singer found peace. He also founded a dynasty that continues to this day.

Hardly a day goes by in my trade that I am not fixing a Singer sewing machine and I sometimes feel that I am operating on Isaac Singer's genius. Some of his early machines, designed as the American Civil War raged almost have his fingerprints on them. As a fellow engineer and master craftsman I see his mind in his mechanics. I see how he solved complex problems to bring us the first practical sewing machine to be used by the masses.

Out of all the sewing machine pioneers that I have written about Isaac Singer's life stands out as simply astounding. Imagine a spider's web that stretches across the globe and in its centre is one man. That man is Isaac Merritt Singer.

They say a few men are touched by fire in their lives; Isaac was one of these men. From the day he was born until the day he died he was a man that stood head and shoulders above the crowd, and not only because he was over six foot five! Nearly a foot taller than the average height of his day.

Although Isaac Merritt Singer claimed to his dying day that he

Before the sewing machine every stitch was made by hand.
The sewing machine not only changed the way we dressed but,
as you will see, it changed our world.

had invented the sewing machine, he did and did not. What the genius did was something far more important, he took the best of what had existed at the time and made something better, the first sewing machine of the age that was guaranteed to work. Isaac had an inventive mind developing a mechanical digging machine for rock excavation, a rock-drilling machine, a grain threshing machine, a woodcarving machine and a printer's letter cutting machine as well as patenting dozens of improvements to sewing machines.

With his best creation, his sewing machine, Isaac Singer and his handpicked men promoted it with such astonishing flare and capability that it became the number one of its kind in the world. Marketing experts today would do well to examine his methods, as they were simply the best. From destroying any opposition to mass give-a-ways and beautiful models, Isaac used every tactic possible to promote his machines.

Isaac Singer and his business partner Edward Clark manipulated the market and built multiple businesses to supply everything from thread to sewing machines and created a truly multinational conglomerate. They then controlled supply and demand with such cold blooded brilliance it resulted in Singer sewing machines dominating the world for generations. If not the first, Isaac Singer was certainly the ultimate capitalist.

Obsession may be too strong a word but for over 30 years I have been carefully collecting and chronologically listing every piece of singer information that I came across. I suppose growing up in the sewing industry it was little surprise, I had been surrounded by Singer sewing machines since a child, even having my nappy changed on a sewing table! Though I thought that I would be the last person who would ever become a nurd it did seem to be true. I had become gripped with anything to do with Isaac Singer. I had helped hundreds of schools, colleges, universities, museums, collectors, magazines and publications all over the globe; I had been on the radio and television all because of this specialist in-depth knowledge that I had sucked up over a lifetime.

Like all of my reference work, used daily around the world, I normally stick to factual dates and figures but as Isaac's story grew it moved away from a statistical theses to more of a factual novel. Isaac's world seemed to come to life, his carefully hidden trail grew as the puzzle came together and eventually the real man leapt from the page.

Let me tell you about the man who became a household name, a forgotten giant who helped forge a modern America long before Titan's like J P Morgan and Henry Ford. The tiny acorn he planted grew into one of the largest companies in the world, affecting millions of people around the globe and heralding in a modern age.

Who would you say is the most famous person you know? We can all name loads and yet amazingly more people on our planet are familiar with the name Singer than Jesus. But why is he so overlooked? I try in the following pages to examine the series of events that led to our capitalist to be excluded from the pages of history.

Isaac Singer was an extraordinary and complicated man. He

grew from a penniless, cunning and devious street-wise kid, living on his wits, to one of the richest men of his time. His character also changed from cold-blooded and ruthless in his youth, to a cheerful benefactor throwing children's parties in his old age. But he never lost his crafty streak, which his last wife would find out to her cost.

When he died the public read the papers with disbelief, with open-mouths and with bulging eyes. How could it be possible that one man, who had come from nothing, almost begging on the streets, had died so rich? And his children! In his will Isaac took the time to name most of them (mothered by various wives and mistresses) leaving more than twenty of them sizable trusts that made them rich in their own right. Isaac's fortune was so vast that it lasted for five generations before its original wealth finally became untraceable.

There is also little doubt that he fathered a host of other children, some he probably never even knew about. Many of his offspring later set Europe ablaze with publicity, scandal and a little intrigue.

I have loved writing this story; it often felt like I was searching for the Scarlet Pimpernel – *"we seek him here, we seek him there"*. His families' elusive trail is full of twists, turns and surprising characters. If ever there was a mini-series that needed filming, from Isadora Duncan to Agatha Christie, this is it. This has to be the best story that never made it to Hollywood.

Please forgive any mistakes. I have had to sift through the innuendo, gossip and downright lies, so be prepared for an

The Paris fashion is to show how much sewing
was in clothes during the 19th century.
Dresses in the picture would have taken months
to make by hand but only days with a sewing machine.

enthusiastic but amateur production with a little touch of poetic licence. Where possible I have included some of the legends and gossip that may have a thread of truth, so it will be for you, my dear reader, to decide. Some of it was just too good not to include!

There are many members of the Singer dynasty alive today and it is my dearest hope not to offend any of them. In fact, whereas the periodicals of the day often painted Isaac as a bigamist and a monster, I have brought to you the facts, not the inflated fiction and bias of the time. Funnily, many of the completely wrong facts I came across were from family members, who have grown their own legends over the years to fit in with their personal family history.

With my Sewalot Website I research most of the early sewing machine pioneers and I am currently chipping away at a large reference book titled *The Sewing Machine Kings*. However the story of Isaac Singer sometimes slips away from a reference book as Isaac's real life goes haywire with crazy incidents that you just couldn't make up. I am sure a great writer like Allison Weir could work her magic on Isaac, like she has so many historical figures, and make a brilliant nail-biting page-turner out of his story.

The Internet has opened up Isaac's life like never before and just about every place, date, and quote of Isaac's life is now scattered amongst the public domain. What I wanted to bring you is far more than just facts and figures, but an easy and enjoyable read that will also appeal to younger readers who may be inspired by Isaac's rags to riches journey.
Long before the great entrepreneurs and capitalists like Rockefeller and Vanderbilt, that today grace parks and museums with their statues, there was Isaac Merritt Singer. While Andrew Carnegie was still an assistant telegraph operator for the Pennsylvanian Railroad, Isaac was well on his way to changing our world. He was in the right place at the

right time and while America was still a fledgling nation it was men like Isaac, the son of an immigrant, who, with strength of character, will and determination, forged the country into the great industrial power that it became. His factories employed men from the Civil War, his products sold universally, making people strive to afford them and in turn improved their lives. I hope that Isaac's brilliance, which eventually brought work to millions, will shine through these pages.

My darling wife Yana said I will have made a few faux pas but I told her that was impossible as that was way too hard to spell!

In this book I have pieced together an amazingly complicated and twisted puzzle with more than a few pieces hidden from us, many by Isaac himself. Please do not take all my dates as gospel. I have travelled countless miles, rubbing gravestones, reviewing patent documents and sifting through endless paperwork and publications to try and prise fact from fiction, yet some accurate dates still elude me.

I hope as more light shines onto this amazing man, and his family, my story will be improved upon, but after decades of collecting information I reached a point where I had to stop accumulating and publish. At the end I give a short list of some of the people and places that have helped.

By now you must be getting fed up with me rambling on, so come with me on a journey that will blow your mind; a journey through one man's fascinating life, a life that really did change our world.

THE SONG OF THE SHIRT
(Thomas Hood)

With fingers weary and worn,
With eyelids heavy and red,
A woman sat, in unwomanly rags,
Plying her needle and thread
Stitch! stitch! stitch!
In poverty, hunger and dirt,
And still, with a voice of dolorous pitch
She sang the 'Song of the Shirt'.

Isaac Merritt Singer distinguished as ever, shown here later in life as one of the world's richest men. Singer's donated this picture to the Smithsonian. It shows Isaac in his favourite smoking jacket. His children loved him wearing it at their palace, Oldway in Paignton, England, as they said it made him look like Father Christmas. He had a touch of red in his hair, was well over six feet five tall, had hypnotic eyes, and was totally irresistible to women.

CHAPTER 1

ISAAC MERRITT SINGER: HIS ROOTS

Isaac Merritt Singer was the youngest of eight children. His father, Adam Singer was probably of German-Jewish origin. I say this as there was a Jewish family in his hometown of Frankfurt, Germany, known as the Reisingers, who were originally of Hungarian origin. There are certainly many Reisingers still in Germany today, especially Bonn, who claim to be descendants of Isaac. But as we shall find out, Isaac's Jewish roots later mixed with Catholic beliefs, and caused quite a few problems in the final days of his life.

Adam Singer's mother was apparently a protestant and one of the reasons Adam may have gone to America was to escape religious pressures from his father. Either way, as he registered in America he removed the 'Rei' and entered the country as Adam Singer.

Some tales say that Isaac Singer's father was a Lutheran who arrived in New York around 1769 at the age of 16. Some say that he was not born until 1772, was married with a daughter Elizabeth and came to America with his first wife in 1803. We know for a fact that he did have a daughter Elizabeth as she married Daniel Colby and is buried Union Rural Cemetery, Oswego. I am sure these discrepancies will be corrected with census details coming to light almost daily.

Either way the German immigrant had arrived in America to chase a dream, and carve a new life out of the wilderness. Little did he know that, out of all his children, his youngest son Isaac would fulfil that dream!

Chapter 2

Give me your tired, your poor, your huddled masses yearning to breathe free
Isabelle Eugenie Boyer

Part 1

Who would believe that even today, people sailing to New York in America set eyes on one of Isaac's wives? Yes, one of the first sights they see when nearing Ellis Island is the Statue of Liberty, which is supposedly modelled on the most beautiful woman in 19th century Europe, Singer's half-French, half-South African wife and actress, Isabelle Eugenie Boyer.

There is a heated debate raging on this point, but let me tell you why all roads point to Isaac's wife.

Gustav Eiffel, of Eiffel Tower fame, built the framework for Bartholdi's Statue of Liberty. It enabled it to stand proud, welcoming people from all over the world. Édouard René de Laboulaye had the idea of presenting a statue representing liberty as a gift to the United States of America. Both Bartholdi and Laboulaye were fascinated with freedom, especially the black struggle for emancipation from slavery that was rumbling on around the world. It is no surprise then that the pair were attracted to the famously widowed Isabella Singer, whose father was from South Africa.

The sculptor Frederic Auguste Bartholdi turned his old friend Laboulaye's idea into reality. After Isaac's death, Isabelle, his last wife, moved back to Paris where she became the toast of the city. Bartholdi knew Isabelle Singer rather well and rumours say that he had a passionate affair with her during his third marriage. Artists, eh!

Bartholdi originally asked his mother to pose for the basic statue just to get the feminine outline, but despite her devotion to her son she could not, or would not stand still enough for long periods. His mother never denied or admitted that she had modelled for her son.

Bartholdi also supposedly asked Jeanne-Emile Baheux de Puysiex to pose for the statue. He had met her while holidaying in America, and she later became his wife. These tricky spellings are giving me a headache! However, she openly reported that she was too shy to allow her face to be used for the statue and never once publically admitted to being the model.

So, in my opinion, after staring at family pictures for years it really was Isabelle Singer, the French actress and innkeeper's daughter, who grew into one of the most flamboyant, beautiful and rich woman in Europe, that finally posed naked for the Statue of Liberty in his Paris studio.

If you take a look at Winnaretta Singer (Isaac and Isabelle's daughter), you will see a resemblance between the faces of her and The Statue of Liberty, especially that unique Singer nose. Winnaretta was the daughter, not the mum who posed for the statue but clear few close up photos of Isabelle exist. Bartholdi was deliberately vague as to who posed for the statue. This would have made sense if he were allegedly having an affair with a married woman!

Lady Liberty was finally placed on Richard Morris Hunt's pedestal in 1886. Originally The Statue of Liberty was a reddish-brown, being made of red copper, but over the years, with exposure to the elements, it has turned green.

Now, if you still are not convinced about Isabella, I shall give you yet another piece of evidence. The front cover and picture on page 25 is part of a poster kindly sent to me by John Domino in Belgium (who currently has one of the 19th century originals). It clearly shows Isabelle and the latest Singer sewing machine of the period. The Singer Company were not silly; such a great advertising scoop was not to be wasted.

Here we see Isabelle radiating from the centre of the poster, surrounded by Singer's achievements. You can't get much more convincing than that, can you?

Singers wasted no time in using The Statue of Liberty in their advertising. Here is one of their French adverts of the period showing Isabelle and the latest Singer sewing machine, with their impressive factory behind.

Let us summarise – Isabelle was the only woman to openly boast about posing for The Statue of Liberty. Apparently tales tell that she would hold her champagne glass up at parties posing as the statue and shout out "Liberty". She was in the right place and with the right people, at the right time. The Singer Company openly used The Statue of Liberty and Isabelle in their advertising, and finally here she is in the poster. As they say, if it walks like a duck and talks like a duck, then it's probably a duck. Of course in that strange way life plays tricks I may be proved wrong, but for now I rest my case M'lord.

CHAPTER 3

THE BEGINNING OF A LEGEND

So now that I have caused a ruckus, let us get back to Isaac Singer and his tale. As we can see, even as an old man, Isaac Singer's charm and wealth attracted beautiful women, and Isabelle was his last conquest. As a young man, by all accounts, he had the devil in him. He was a renowned womanizer and father to at least two-dozen children by wives and lovers. However, I am jumping ahead. He had many miles to go and many hardships to face before he made his millions, built palaces, and chased petticoats.

Isaac Singer's father, Adam Singer, set up business as a wheelwright, millwright and barrel maker, or cooper, in Troy, New York. In 1788, he married a younger American girl, Ruth Benson, whose family had originally migrated to America from Holland in the 1680's. Isaac later named one of his many children Ruth.

History tells us that Adam may have lived until 1855. He was 102 (or more likely 83 going by some dates). Either way it is an amazing fact for the hard frontier life of those days. It may be true even without porridge, yoghurt and wheat germ cereals!

According to history books, Isaac Singer was born in one of several potential locations in the New York area. As he has become more famous, several of them have claimed the prodigal son as their own, but I have yet to discover the actual written proof (which will hopefully turn up one day).

For our story we will go for the two most likely towns of Isaac's birth. Some say Isaac Singer was born in the small frontier town of Schaghticoke, NY, on the 26th or 27th October 1811. Others say he was born in Johnsonville, a hamlet of Pittstown, Rensselaer County, New York.

Either way his dad Adam decided to move his family to Granby, Oswego where Isaac spent his childhood.

Adam and Ruth Singer seem to have had six boys and possibly two girls, eight kids in all – these are the ones that I have found details of:

John Valentine Singer, born 1791, died 1887.
Alexander Singer, born around 1800, died?
Elizabeth Singer, born 1801, died 1872.
Christiana Singer, born 1804, died 1887.
Isaac Merritt Singer, born 1811, died 1875.
Elijah Singer, born 1813, died 1860.

John Singer left home early and went to sea. Many years later he found Isaac, who had just invented his sewing machine. Isaac, ever the persuasive actor, managed to wriggle John's savings out of him, which he used to finance his invention. John Singer asked for his money back twice, though I never found out if he was ever rewarded.

Isaac's mother, Ruth, divorced Adam Singer in 1821 and left the family home when Isaac was just 10 (some say earlier, but 10 suits the children's dates). She may have gone off to return to her Quaker roots in Albany, leaving Isaac's father to run his business, and try and bring up eight children on his own. There was a rumour that Adam Singer had an affair and it was the last straw for Ruth, who found out after overhearing gossip at a Sunday church meeting. She immediately confronted him, packed her pony and trap and left.

It is said that in later years, Adam Singer went to find Ruth, possibly to tell her of the fortune their youngest son was making. He tracked her down in Albany, NY, only to find that she had passed away shortly before his arrival.

Although Isaac's family had moved away it would be back in New York City, many years later, that Isaac Singer made an indelible mark on American history, leading to one of the first multinational companies and eventually to one of the first skyscrapers and largest buildings in the world at that time.

It was not long before Adam found another wife, and it is said that Isaac never connected with his stepmother. Hard frontier life, working to keep the family afloat and broken marriages may explain why Isaac never had proper schooling – he must have had a hard childhood for, within two years of Ruth leaving, aged just 12 he slipped on his running shoes and ran as far away from home as he could.

Chapter 4

1823

There is little detail of Isaac's early years away from home. It must have been hard on the road at such a tender age; what would make a child run from home is anybody's guess. He probably stayed with some of his older brothers who had left home earlier and were living in Rochester. Or did he? Isaac hardly ever talked about his early childhood.

Some tales tell that Isaac ran away with a travelling carnival that was passing through his town. Isaac loved the carnival and it was probably sitting in the audience as a young man that he first caught the acting bug. We do know that carnivals regularly moved around his part of the country, entertaining the outlying towns that had limited amusement away from the big cities.

So if he did indeed stow away it is possible that when he was found they let him stay with the troop, earning his board and keep as they moved from town to town. Was it this travelling that made Isaac have ants in his pants? Our man never seemed to stop travelling throughout his life until his final home shortly before his death many years later.

A carnival was the perfect training ground for an inventor. Carnivals are like ships at sea, they need to contain and make everything out on the road. Here Isaac would have gained precious knowledge on how to make do and to mend.

Sincere's *History Of The Sewing Machine* states that Isaac eventually worked his way up from basic help as a pitchman and gofer to roustabout and finally, just before he left the carnival, he would introduce the acts in the big tent.

There are also tales that during his travelling period, he worked part-time as a woodworker, carpenter, joiner, and lathe operator, paying for his own rudimentary schooling between jobs until he was 19.

So how did the most famous name in the sewing world get into the sewing business? We shall find out later, but for now our young runaway has caught the acting bug.

Isaac Singer was smart, cunning and ruthless. He had to be to survive on the streets of 19th century America. The country was a bustling mass of humanity at the time with immigrants flooding in and prosperity blooming. There were endless opportunities for those willing to grasp them.

"A Horse! A horse! My kingdom for a horse"

While on a long stopover in Rochester, Isaac learnt how to read (but not write properly), and found a fondness for Shakespeare.

Isaac was a born showman and it became his life's passion. He thought of himself as an accomplished actor, landing himself amongst other early parts, the role of Richard III with a Rochester group when he was still under 20. Now well built, six foot five inches tall with blonde-red hair, he was an imposing young man. He played his parts so well that he even toured with them for a while.

Chapter 5

Isaac's First Wife
Catherine Maria Haley

In December of 1830, Isaac, still only 19, married Catherine Maria Haley from Palmyra who was 15. Isaac went to live with her parents who were from Croton Landing (Croton on the Hudson) in Westchester County. Isaac soon left to work with George Pomeroy near Fly Creek in Otsego County and regularly rode to the Cooperstown Post Office to send money back to Catherine. Some say that it was here that he first bumped into Edward Clark, his future partner.

In 1834, when Isaac was 23, his first son William was born, possibly in a house in Port Gibson.

William Singer was later to fill in many details of his father and grandfather's sketchy lives. It appears that Isaac would work at almost any job during the day and try his hand on the stage in the evening.

By 1836 Isaac and family were living in New York. He had

learned the trades of mechanic and cabinetmaker at Hoe's Press, possibly in Waterloo, New York. It was a combination of these trades that would later combine to allow him to understand the complexities of the sewing machine. But Isaac was always drawn back to acting and soon joined up with another travelling band of actors, sending money home to Catherine when he could.

Chapter 6

The Baltimore Strolling Players

Now we pop back to Baltimore, for there are already problems brewing with Isaac's love life. As a handsome, tall young man away from home Isaac was trying to eke out a living as an actor, supplementing his wages with almost any trade. Isaac moved with the Baltimore Players, working during the day in any paid trade and in the evening helping as a handyman and part-time performer. That was until he set eyes on Mary Ann Sponsler.

It was at one of his performances in Baltimore that he spied a young beauty in the audience. She was the bright-eyed daughter of a Baltimore oyster trader and before long he had used all his charms on the eighteen year old. Before long Isaac had moved in with her parents, probably failing to mention his wife and children in New York! Charles Sponsler, Mary Ann's brother joined the acting entourage with Isaac and many years later became a successful agent for Singer sewing machines, staying out of his sister's later squabbles with the future sewing machine king.

Mary Ann was smitten and took acting classes. She also joined

Isaac on the road; that was until the Baltimore Strolling Players disbanded. Around that time Isaac returned to his family in New York and rather than divorce Catherine, made her pregnant again! Sweet mama…

Mary Ann also moved to New York around September of 1836. Isaac spilt the beans on his earlier marriage to Catherine, but swore it was all over and as soon as he could he would marry her. Wow, I have never heard that one before! This early pledge of marriage was going to come back and haunt him many years later when Mary Ann went on the warpath.

For 25 years Mary Ann had Isaac's children and assumed the titles of Mrs Merritt and Mrs Singer. By all accounts their relationship was passionate and tempestuous.

Just a few months later in 1837 a daughter was born to Catherine; a girl, Lillian C. Singer. It's likely that not long after Catherine found out about Mary Ann, for she then returned with her children, to the family home in Palmyra and later settled in Long Island.

Many years later Isaac paid out a huge sum to officially divorce her, but after Isaac's death Catherine caused a lot more trouble, so we shall be hearing more of her later.

Mary Ann Sponsler would go on to have 10 children with Isaac, their first in July of 1837 (the same year as his wife Catherine had Lillian). Isaac called his son with Mary Ann, Augustus.

Mary Ann always claimed that she was 'morally and in

principle' married to Isaac, though Isaac was already married. Years later she would try and destroy Isaac in court, and while doing so, seemed to tell as many 'porkies' as he did.

Two of Mary Ann and Isaac's children tragically died in infancy, which was not uncommon in that harsh period. In later years Mary Ann became a huge thorn in Isaac's side and even after his death she also caused uproar, selling her story to the tabloids and holding up probate in court for months, saying she was still his legitimate wife. However in the early years together they were deeply in love and bitterness was a long way off.

It was around this time that papers of the day put Isaac in Chicago where he supposedly invented a reaping machine for harvesting grain. I have never managed to trace the machine but we do know that Isaac was inventing and selling his ideas to pay for his acting.

In 1838 we find Isaac Singer, at the age of 27, working with his brother on the Lockport, Illinois and Michigan Canal.

By the following year in 1839 he used all his ingenuity and skill to invent a machine for drilling and excavating rock. He probably came up with the idea as he, and hundreds more, were manually breaking and shifting tons of rubble with little more than spades and pickaxes. He eventually sold his invention complete with patent rights for a staggering $2,000. It must have been a good invention to command several years' wages.

Chapter 7

The Merritt Players

Isaac quickly put his newfound wealth to use and followed his first love – acting.

Isaac Singer, now 28, formed a group of actors called *The Merritt Players* and they travelled around the country, 'treading the boards'. Apparently, during performances he announced himself as Isaac Merritt of the Merritt Players.

By 1840, Isaac, and his troupe were on the road. Boy, did that man love travelling!

Mary Ann's acting lessons had paid off and she played many of the female roles, headlining as 'Mrs Merritt'. Acting was a hard life and as a travelling band there must have been a lot of cost involved.

Harry Watkins, one of the Merritt Players once noted that on one rainy night the house was pretty much empty and they only took $2.

To Isaac this didn't matter, he was doing what he loved most and as long as he had money, the show would go on.

After their shows they would pack up their buckboards and wagons and head for the next town. It was real frontier life and Isaac adored it. He would set up camp, the family would cook supper around the fire and he would perform his plays as the sun set. It was an idyllic time, but as Isaac toured so his family grew and his finances dwindled. On the 4th of January 1840 Isaac and Mary Ann Sponsler saw the arrival of Violetta Theresa Singer.

Violetta Theresa Singer

Violetta Theresa Singer later married William Fash Proctor in 1862. He had joined the Singer Company in 1853 and worked his way up from the shop floor, originally training as a machinist. Eventually he became Vice President, respectable and wealthy. In the early days of Isaac's sewing machine business, Isaac had seen how besotted Violetta was with William and actively encouraged his fast promotion through the ranks of the company. His following rise in wealth meant that he could look after Violetta in a manner that Isaac approved of. Violetta was subsequently left nothing in Isaac's will. Theresa Singer died at the age of 73 on December 14th 1913.

Chapter 8

1843

1843 was a big year for Isaac; his son, John Albert arrived and Isaac ran out of his invention money.

Singer could charm the socks off anyone, as one hotel manager from Piqua, Ohio, once remembered. Isaac, his partner Mary Ann, and children arrived at his hotel almost penniless. Isaac talked his way into getting rooms and later performed for the guests to pay for their food and board. Tuttle, the hotel owner even allowed Isaac to talk him and his wife out of their own larger family rooms!

When the family packed to leave, the hotelier even gave them a few dollars to help them on their way. He last saw the family heading out of town into the wilderness, on a crammed buckboard pulled by an old nag.

A year later in 1844, daughter Fannie Elizabeth popped out, almost onto the stage! Isaac and Mary Ann found a niche market in performing temperance plays in churches for which they collected a menial payment. I don't expect they happened to mention that they were not married!

It is a fact that for the first 15 years of their time together, Isaac and Mary lived a happy hand-to-mouth existence bringing up their children any way they could. On more than one occasion Isaac would pawn his goods, even his buckboard or wagon to pay for food and lodgings, but all along he somehow kept the show going.

It was not long before Isaac's money ran out completely, and now with children in tow, Isaac reluctantly decided to find regular work. The Merritt Players was finally disbanded in Fredericksburg.

CHAPTER 9

Isaac was soon back making a living from his old trades. His first attempt at the American dream had failed but he was not finished, not by a long way.

In Fredericksburg, PA, at the factory where he worked, Isaac Singer's inventive mind was at work again, this time inventing a machine that automatically carved wooden blocks for printer's type, used in newspapers and books. It automatically cut out letters for a printing press, a laborious job which he was being paid to do manually. It was obviously too expensive or not that successful because even with all of Isaac's powers of persuasion and some partners who had invested in it, he never managed to sell it.

In a statement made many years later, Isaac lightly said that although his printers invention made superior 'type', his partners did not! And so he dissolved the business. This piece of our jigsaw puzzle may or may not be true; however what we do know is that all these little experiences in his life were leading up to his greatest achievement, the Singer sewing machine.

Isaac Singer was a practical man, a workaholic and a man with vision but he had a poor academic education. As a child he only went to school when his father had time and money. This was mainly in the winter, when Isaac attended a common school. Later he paid for his own schooling. His writing shows how much difficulty he had spelling even the simplest words.

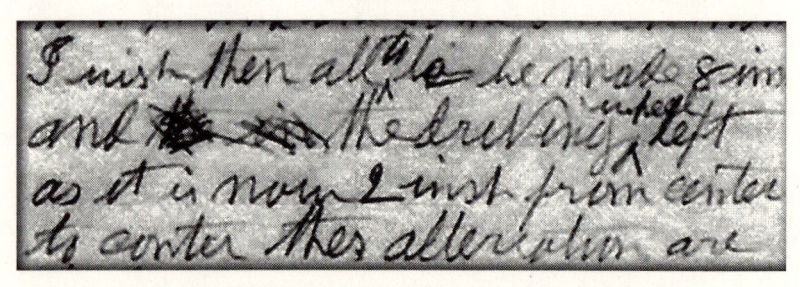

A rare sample of Isaac Singer's poor writing from 1868, showing five corrections in three short lines.

This however did not slow the master showman down. His intellect was undeniable, even as a teenager he was able to quote great chunks of Shakespeare at the drop of a hat. Always one for smooth talking, the handsome young actor and inventor '*wheeled and dealed*' his way through life, while his lover Mary, patched his clothes and cooked his meals.

By 1846 Isaac was in Pittsburgh, trying to develop a new woodcarving machine while continuing to perfect his printing invention. It was here that both Jasper Hamlet and Mary Olive were born.

In 1848 we find our man back in New York where he rented a studio workshop to work on his inventions.

By 1849 he was joined once more by Mary Ann. She moved their children into a low cost rental on Lower East Side and was openly using the name Mrs Singer.

However disaster was to strike. Apparently, in February of 1850 Isaac's inventions were destroyed when a boiler exploded in the unit he was using in Hague Street, which was owned by A B Taylor.

The explosion was said to be so fierce that 60 people were killed and many more injured. Isaac was home (possibly at 130 East 27th Street) with Mary Ann and the children when the explosion happened. When he heard of the disaster he rushed to his premises only to find the place in ruins, bodies everywhere, and his machines in tatters.

Luckily his friend William Proctor had survived and even luckier for Isaac was that his new acquaintance, George B Zieber was fine. Zieber was the man who would change Isaac's life forever.

Chapter 10

George B Zieber

George B Zieber was a printer and publisher of some repute, and had recently published books like *Blue Beard* and *Jack the Giant Slayer* with his publishing arm G B Zieber & Co.

By 1850 George Zieber had talked Isaac Singer into going to the centre of the book trade, Boston, to sell his printing inventions. Here Isaac rented a basement at 19, Harvard Place, and tried once more to sell an interest in his original printing invention, but again failed to find a buyer.

Completely off topic, but a possible connection and very interesting, 1850 was the same year that Jacob Singer, a possible relative of Isaac, set off with John Hodge on an epic 2,300 mile journey across America to the gold fields of California. Jacob Singer joined the famous 49'ers and along with 100,000 other men searched for gold in the streams and gullies of the Golden State. It was a hard life and many men died, many returned penniless, and just a few came back rich.

Now back to our budding inventor. George Zieber and Isaac

had sparked up an immediate friendship at Taylor's and even better for Isaac, George had money. Zieber had witnessed Isaac's mind at work, seen his inventions and he also thought that there was a market for an automatic woodcarving and block-printing machine. Being in printing himself, he probably understood its possibilities better than most, and thought that if Isaac could build it, he could sell it.

George and Isaac would often travel home to New York and stay with Mary in their shabby apartment, where they would have supper and talk of better times ahead. George saw huge potential in Isaac and was willing to invest in him.

George then found workshops at the Woorall Brothers' yard in Worth Street, where Isaac concentrated on rebuilding his carving and cutting machine. As soon as it was ready they headed for the most likely places in Boston to sell their invention. Unfortunately after weeks of appointments and demonstrations not one order followed.

Chapter 11

Orson C Phelps

Unperturbed by their lack of success, in 1850 Isaac and George started renting a basement in Boston from a machine repairer and manufacturer called Phelps. They would work on improving their wood machine but fate was guiding Isaac into a different venture that would make him gloriously rich.

Amongst many trades, Orson Phelps was a scientific instrument maker of considerable skill. While in School Street, Boston, he had even advised sewing machine inventor Elias Howe on his machine way back in 1845 (Elias patented his machine in 1846). Phelps did not see potential in the machine. Actually, he had not completely figured out what the instrument did because Elias was so guarded about it!

At 19 Harvard Place, Phelps made and repaired (not very good) sewing machines under licence for Blodgett & Lerow, who had patented their sewing machine in October of 1849. To begin with, few of the early sewing machine makers really saw the huge potential that sewing machines had. However the new-fangled machines that almost hypnotically joined pieces of fabric together fascinated Isaac. In Isaac's mind this was the invention of the century – all he had to do was make it work properly.

Both Blodgett and Lerow had told Isaac there was no money in sewing machines except selling the licences for others to try and make or sell them. Their machines were notoriously poor with only one in ten being fit for purpose; they were more interested in the selling scam rather than improving their machine and making it work properly. One fascinating thing that they had on their machine (that I have never seen elsewhere) is a shuttle that went round in a circle, whereas all others moved back and forth or side to side. Well, I thought it was fascinating!

Isaac simply smiled when he talked with both Blodgett and Lerow, for he knew their machines were no good and the real market was with a reliable machine that was fit for public use.

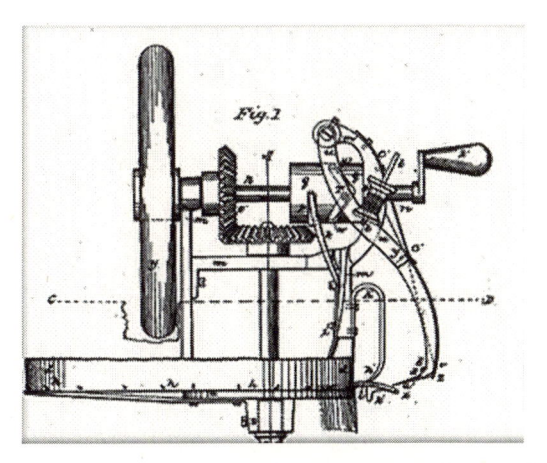

The Blodgett & Lerow sewing machines patented 2 October of 1849 (Pat 6766). The machines were not capable of reliable sewing and constantly failed during use.

Phelps and Singer continually had to fix the machines that the tailors were using (on the top floor above the workshops) so they knew all too well how useless they were. Sherburne C Blodgett's invention was crude and prickly, using points and pins so that any operator soon ended up bleeding and cursing rather than actually sewing anything.

When busy, Phelps would get Singer to repair many of the sewing machines. Isaac was happy to work off some of his rent by repairing them. He was also happy to ingratiate himself into Phelps's setup, someone who had little capital behind him but had a great workshop with skilled staff.

It is a fact that in 1850, very few sewing machines sewed well. It was right back at the birth of the sewing machine industry and some of the ideas just did not work.

While working on the faulty machines in the late summer of 1850, it became clear to Singer's inventive mind that improvements were necessary and he was the man who could carry them out, often boasting to the other engineers in the workshop that he could make a better machine than any he had ever come across.

Isaac would later put his talent where his mouth was. Now, remember that Isaac had no takers for his wood machines. He was obviously hoping for another windfall like with his rock-driller before, but it wasn't happening. If Boston, the centre of the wood trade wasn't interested who would be? Zieber was still reluctantly lending Isaac money to send home to his wife and kids in New York, but by this point, had sunk a large amount into the wood machines with no return.

I bet there is some plans for the machines somewhere. Apparently one of them could do the work of 20 men, and produce better work too!

Chapter 12

The Famous Bet

While Isaac was in a state of despair, his life was about to change forever. He was temporarily staying at the Wilde's Hotel, sharing a room with Zieber and scribbling out drawings of sewing machines. Each time they looked a little better and Zieber was keen to get Isaac onto manufacturing them.

Legend goes that a bet between the two men is what put Isaac on his path to millions.

Zieber needed to encourage Isaac into physically making a sewing machine – for weeks they had been joking about a sewing machine but no action was taking place. He had already quietly written down an equal split contract between Singer, Phelps and himself on a rough piece of paper.

On the 18th of September 1850 Zieber had the paper in his pocket. He was almost out of money and while he had some property he had limited liquid assets. The idea of the deal was that Zieber would pay for the patent and materials, Phelps the workshop and any technical help and Isaac would be the inventive genius that made it all possible.

Isaac would build an improved sewing machine, call it the Jenny Lind and patent it. All future dividends would be split equally amongst the three partners, and so on. Phelps and his staff would also manufacture the future machines.

Zieber kept ribbing Isaac about the sewing machine idea and in the end Isaac boasted once more that he could build a better sewing machine than anything on the market in a matter of days.

At that moment George Zieber leapt up and told him to put his genius where his mouth was, and Isaac said he would take the bet if he had any money. Zieber, unperturbed, offered to lend him the money as long as they shared any profit from the machine if he produced it! When Singer agreed, Zieber quickly pulled out his contract, found a witness, James Baker Junior, and got a laughing Isaac to sign. The deal was struck!

Forty dollars was the bet, and it was that $40 that would make Isaac Singer one of the richest men in the world.

Zieber and Phelps were onto a good thing. If Isaac Singer did make a sewing machine that worked well then they would get their money back and much more. If Isaac failed then Zieber would get Isaac to work his debt off over the next few months and stop trying to flog his wood machines that were driving all three of them mad!

Isaac Singer was fired up and had been handed just enough

money to have a go at making a practical sewing machine, something that, in the entire history of the world, had not yet been done.

Supposedly ignorant of many of the patents of the time, Isaac Singer went to work building the machine that would revolutionise manufacturing and, as the periodicals of the day later said, 'set women free'.

I'm very suspicious that Isaac built his machine from scratch in 11 days – the casting of the sewing machine body alone would be a mammoth task, let alone machining out all the bearing supports and so on. Elias Howe took many months to build just one of his machines. What Isaac did have was all the spare

Elias Howe is considered to be the inventor of the first lock-stitch sewing machine which he patented in 1846. Elias had a troubled time selling his brilliant but complicated machine and resorted to making his fortune by suing anyone who infringed on his patents. This woodcut was made shortly before his death at the tender age of 48, you can see that he was exhausted by his struggles.

sewing machine parts from broken machines in Phelps' workshop. It would not surprise me if he used some of the pieces to build his initial model, and remember that Phelps had seen Elias Howe's machine!

Anyway, whatever the truth of the matter, Isaac was on his way to his first sewing machine.

Incidentally, there were plenty of sewing machines around in 1850 but none that were, like Isaac's, reliable, with a guarantee! The public would later know and trust that. Men had tried through the ages to make a good sewing machine but all had shortcomings. The major mistake most of them made was to copy the hand movement of a sewer, rather than invent an entirely new method as Elias Howe did in 1846.

CHAPTER 13

History is Made

At last, in a basement workshop, a gifted 39-year-old man was in the process of building the first practical sewing machine – a man who still had a passion to make a fortune and, of course, win his bet with Zieber.

Isaac's improvements to the sewing machine, like the straight needlebar, the flat bed to support the cloth, the rotating pin-wheel to feed the fabric through and the sprung presser foot to press the material down onto the revolving pin-wheel were all going to make Isaac Singer one of the richest men of the Victorian era.

Isaac had told Phelps and Zieber that there were ten principle motions that made a reliable sewing machine. Unfortunately for him many of them had already been patented, like the shuttle from Elias Howe.

Now let's look at what Isaac knew about sewing machines in 1850. In September of that year the sixth annual exhibition of the Massachusetts Charitable Mechanic's Association was held at the Faneuil and Quincy Halls in Boston. On show was a rotary hook sewing machine made by A B Wilson and four other sewing engines or machines. Isaac would have gone to the show, if only to try and sell his wood carving machine, but also being an engineer he would not have missed the opportunity to see what was going on, especially with the sewing machines.

We know that Isaac was familiar with other sewing machines, like the Blodgett & Lerow ones that he repaired for Phelps. We know that Phelps had seen the Elias Howe model and finally we know that Isaac was already an accomplished engineer and inventor. All these add up to making Isaac the perfect man to invent the first practical sewing machine in the world. And boy was the world ready and waiting.

Isaac Singer's future versions of events were naturally flamboyant. In later life he often told the tale of biblical proportions of how he worked tirelessly for eleven days and eleven nights building his sewing machine. How he went without food and grabbed only a few moments sleep. And how his invention would save women from their endless toil.

That may be true. Whatever the story, the result was undeniable, a sewing machine that actually sewed a reliable lockstitch over and over again.

Isaac Singer's own words

"My attention was first directed to sewing machines late in August, 1850. I then saw in Boston some Blodgett sewing

machines, which Mr. Orson C. Phelps was employed to keep in running order. I had then patented a carving machine, and Phelps, I think, suggested that if I could make the sewing machine practical I should make money.

Considering the matter over night, I became satisfied I could make them practically applicable to all kinds of work and the next day showed Phelps and George B. Zieber a rough sketch of the machine I proposed to build. It contained a table to support the cloth horizontal instead of a feed-bar from which was suspended vertically in the Blodgett machine, a vertical presser-foot to hold the cloth, and an arm to hold the presser-foot and needlebar over the table. I explained to them how the work was to be fed over the table and under the presser-foot, by a wheel having short pins on its periphery projecting through a slot in the table, so that the work would be automatically caught, fed, and freed from the pins, in place of attaching and detaching the work to and from the baster-plate by hand, as was necessary in the Blodgett machine.

Phelps and Zieber were satisfied that it would work. I had no money. Zieber offered forty dollars to build a model machine. Phelps offered his best endeavours to carry out my plan and make the model in his shop. If successful we were to share equally. I worked at it day and night, sleeping but three or four hours out of the twenty-four, and eating generally but once a day, as I knew I must make it for the forty dollars, or not get it at all.

The machine was completed in eleven days. About nine o'clock in the evening we got the parts together, and tried it. It did not sew. Exhausted with almost unremitting work, they pronounced it a failure, and left me one by one until only Zieber was with me.

Zieber held the lamp, and I continued to try the machine but anxiety and incessant work had made me nervous, and I could not get tight stitches. Sick at heart, about midnight we started for our hotel. On the way we sat down on a pile of boards, and Zieber mentioned that the loose loops of thread were on the upper side of the cloth. It flashed upon me that we had forgotten to adjust the tension on the needle-thread.

We went back, adjusted the tension, tried the machine, and it sewed five stitches perfectly, then the thread snapped. But that was enough to secure my forty dollars."

An original woodcut from Isaac's description of events.

The rest, as they say is history. What Isaac did not mention was that over those few days, as he instructed the other engineers like Jott Grant on what to make, he was very tense, often exploding in exasperation when an idea failed. To balance these outbursts, which were always short lived with Isaac, he would act out some of his old plays for the workmen in an improvised one-man show.

The actual machine was put together away from prying eyes in a separate office.

One little point of interest I mentioned earlier is that the first sewing machine sold by Isaac Singer was going to be named The Jenny Lind, after Isaac's infatuation with the beautiful Swedish singing sensation. She was touring America with the P T Barnum show as Isaac was finishing his machine.

However, Isaac thought that his sewing machine may outlast Jenny, who would soon be returning home and so it was the British manufacturer, William Campion who named one of his Nottingham models, The Jenny Lind Sewing Machine. Zieber later told tales that it was he that persuaded Isaac to call his machine Singer, but I doubt if Isaac needed much persuasion.

After a few minor hiccups Isaac Singer's machine worked and the men started to make extra models to sell. Isaac's machine was soon advertised in the Boston journals and the three men waited with baited breath to see if any orders came in.

CHAPTER 14

Isaac and Phelps often argued furiously about under whose name the patent should be filed. Zieber looked on but kept quiet, taking Isaac's side. Isaac then calmed everything down and went back to work constructing more machines until September of 1850. Once the coast was clear Isaac made up an excuse that he was taking one of his models to show some friends, but in fact what he did was pack up his sewing machine and head for the patent office in New York. Zieber was in on the plan and had given Isaac his last few dollars for the patent application and his travelling expenses.

Once there, Isaac hired the services of Charles M Keller, who drew up plans for Isaac's patent application and also wrote the description in longhand as Isaac dictated it (remember, Isaac was a poor writer).

'To all whom it may concern: Be it known that I, Isaac Merritt Singer of the City, County and State of New York have invented certain new and useful improvements in the machine for sewing seams in cloth.'

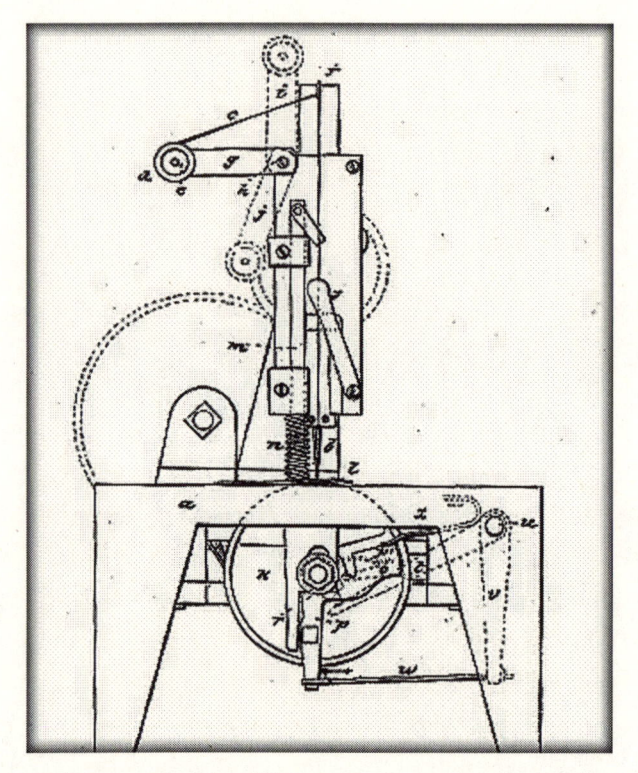

The original patent drawing of Singer's sewing machine patent 8294, 12 August 1851. The patent was not granted full patent protection until 29 September 1856 because of one of the largest court battles in American history.

Against all the odds Isaac Singer had come up with the first reliable and practical sewing machine in history with only his name on the patent!

Isaac managed to get back to Mary Ann by 6 October 1850, just as she was giving birth to their son Charles Alexander. Ever the salesman, Isaac tried to sell one of his machines to the doctor! Sadly, Charles died when he was just four.

Some time later, Isaac got down to work; improving his pressure feed mechanism until he came up with a satisfactory wheel feed that rolled the cloth through with the correct pressure. Under Isaac's instructions Phelps's men were making prototype after prototype until he got the mechanism spot on. He then rushed back to Keller to get that in the patented queue as well. The second patent was issued 13 April 1852.

Later in the year it became clear to Isaac that Phelps was in the

Well folks, this is what it is all about, the first really practical sewing machine in the world. It had many ideas, a straight vertical moving needle going up-and-down (copied) and a sprung presser foot that applied pressure to the work as it went under the foot. It also had a wheel that fed the work through, and a shuttle (copied from Elias Howe). Boy that was going to lead to trouble…The machine was supposedly built by hand in 11 days… umm, I doubt it. Even with a dedicated team it would have taken months, but the courts would ultimately decide who was telling the whole truth.

way. In Isaac's mind he had contributed little to the machine and when it started to sell, would want a third of the profits. Phelps was finally bullied and bought out of the flimsy partnership with the help of a new partner bringing money in, one Barzillan Ransom. Ransom was a manufacturer of bags and instantly saw the potential of Isaac's machine. A bitter Phelps was taken on as a salesman. It was a decision he later dearly regretted and, as we shall find out, led him to attack Singer in the courts.

Now I must add a little note here – while all this was going on Isaac was having his old wandering-eye problems with women, for 1851 was not only the year that Isaac patented the first good sewing machine in history, but also the year that Mary Eastwood Walters (another Mrs Merritt) produced a child by Isaac, a daughter named Alice. I believe Mary Eastwood had been hired to demonstrate Isaac's machine but soon fell under his spell while he was demonstrating how to use the treadle mechanism, and it would seem that one thing led to another!

Chapter 15

From this point on in our history, true mass production of clothes and many other industries was about to start. You can look back on many items from lamps to typewriters and see their birth in mass production from around 1851.

An example:
Late in 1851 or early in 1852, a shoemaker name John Brooke Nichols, seeing the potential in the new sewing machines bought a Howe sewing machine and tried and convert it to sew leather for his business. This failed so he purchased a machine from Isaac Singer, and ultimately managed to successfully alter the Singer machine to sew leather. Nichols then proceeded to offer the rights, via Isaac Singer, to shoe manufacturers such as John Wooldredge and George Keene in Essex County.

The Goodyear Welt Stitcher and the McKay Sole Stitcher soon followed. This introduced a new era of mechanised mass production in the shoe industry. The future was here!

Now back to Isaac Singer and his search for wealth.
Barzillan Ransom (I love that name) was supposed to have invested a colossal $10,000 in Isaac and George's company,

which allowed not only the buyout of Phelps, but also the instant expansion of the business.

They immediately opened premises in New York at the back of Smith & Conant's at 256 Broadway. The story goes that Isaac went to rent rooms at the business but ended up selling them two sewing machines and fitting out his son, William, with a new suit for free! You have to admire the man.

Thomas Jones was then hired to look after the back store. He made some makeshift tables where he and Singer's other son, Gus, sat and waited for orders. Gus, who was 14, was an excellent young engineer, even helping his dad with improvements to the sewing machine. Mistakes did happen however – one day in the store, Gus had the tip of one of his fingers cut off after he got it caught during a machine demonstration!

Jones later took a sewing machine out on the road in the back of a cart to go and find some orders in the surrounding suburbs. Meanwhile another cheap rental shop was acquired over the railway depot where machines could also be demonstrated and stored.

All the machines were still being made at Phelps's premises, though he himself was now forced out on the road selling the machine. Actually just about everyone was out on the road selling sewing machines including William, Isaac's oldest son.

Isaac quickly settled into improving his machine. Later in 1851, Isaac had seen that Barzillan was more talk than walk, and given that he had not coughed up most of the promised $10,000, Isaac set about bullying Ransom out of the business. In fact Barzillan Ransom was not a well man (probably not helped by Isaac's abuse), and after advice from his son, he agreed to leave the partnership and settled for payment in sewing machines (that he could sell to recoup his investment). He died shortly after leaving the firm.

Now only Zieber and Singer were left as partners in the I M Singer & Co business. Zieber had little idea at the time that Isaac would turn on him as well.

THE SINGER MACHINE, AUGUST 12, 1851.
Earliest model filed in Patent Office. Reproduced from the SCIENTIFIC AMERICAN of November 1, 1851.

CHAPTER 16

Singer's biggest problem with his superb machine was that he had infringed several patents while putting it together. His worst nightmare came true when he found himself in court against one of the most powerful men in America, the stubborn and driven, Elias Howe.

Elias Howe had come from nothing, even attending his young wife's funeral in a borrowed suit, to become a wealthy man. He had successfully been charging all the other sewing machine manufacturers for the use of his 1846 patents and Isaac Singer, the upstart, was going to be no exception.

In James Parton's *'History of the Sewing Machine'*, written in 1872, Parton took the side of Elias Howe. He states, "*Mr Singer had not been long in the business before he was reminded by Elias Howe that he was infringing on his patent. The adventurer threw all his energy, and his growing means, into the contest against the original inventor.*" Although Howe had a rocky start in the sewing machine business, he made most of his money suing everyone who had infringed on his patents.

Elias Howe's machine looked nothing like Isaac Singer's but it had the Howe patents that Singer may have copied.

Chapter 17

The Cunning Isaac & Edward Clark

Isaac Singer no longer really needed his final partner, Zieber, he needed a legal brain. Firstly to fight his court case with Elias Howe, and secondly, to figure out how more people could afford his expensive machine. If he could come up with a way to make his machine cheaper he could start a fire that no one could put out. However, as much as he tried he could not do it, so his market remained industrial; that was until Edward Clark came along.

Now we have to back-peddle a little and introduce the fascinating Edward Clark.

He was the exact opposite to Singer; he was a man of medium build with a large nose upon which sat his rectangular reading spectacles. He had a shaved face but wore a beard under his chin up to his ears. He covered his receding hair with a wig and was the typical sort of person that you may have found hunched over a desk in some legal office. However that is where the façade ends, for behind the piercing periwinkle blue eyes of Edward Clark was a huge intellect and an even bigger ambition.

Edward Clark.

Clark was born in Athens, Greene County, New York on 19 December 1811. He graduated from Williams College in 1830 and went to work for the legal firm of Ambrose Jordan.

He worked his way up and became a partner of New York lawyers. Around 1848, Jordan, Clark & Co was approached by Isaac Singer to try and earn some money out of his inventions. Clark instantly saw huge potential in the new sewing machine venture, even agreeing to swap some of his services for a part share in Isaac's failed wood machine, just so he could get involved.

Though Clark had been disappointed in Isaac's wood machine he saw the huge possibilities ahead and became a much closer acquaintance, especially when orders for sewing machines started rolling in.

Isaac Singer was desperately in need of investment in his expanding business and was also up to his neck in debts and legal actions. For help with his problems, Isaac offered Clark some of the rights in his patent rather than money.

Isaac and Clark talked to Zieber and they all agreed a three-way split of the business. From this point on there was Isaac Singer, Edward Clark and George Zieber running the fledgling Singer Company, but that was all going to change!

Allegedly, as early as June of 1851, Isaac and Clark had quietly decided that there was no reason to have Zieber as a partner and if the opportunity arose, he would be removed as efficiently as possible, leaving just the two budding capitalists as sole equal partners.

As the business grew all three partners got stuck in with the daily grind of empire building. Clark handled all the legal matters; Isaac handled machine improvements, development and a string of patents, (and unfortunately the hiring of female staff!) Zieber managed general operations. Isaac told later in one of his court actions that by June of 1865 Singer's had made over 132,389 various sewing machines. It showed the astonishing growth of a brand new industry that came from nothing, which had to be set up step by step from specially fabricated manufacturing machines to agencies.

In the background Isaac and Clark were waiting for the opportunity to remove Zieber.

One morning early in March 1852 Edward Clark called on the

workshop. He wanted to see the order book and how the machines were progressing. Zieber got the wind up and figured that Clark and Singer were up to something and stormed around to Isaac's house, now on East Fifth Street. Zieber was intent on cementing properly their precarious agreements and legally securing his cut of the patent. After all it had only been possible because of his constant support!

Zieber almost pushed his way by Mary Ann and the children, and rushed up to Isaac's bedroom, where Isaac was still half asleep. Zieber starting explaining his concerns, but Isaac interrupted him and finally told him the truth. Isaac wanted Zieber out and his verbal agreements would be worthless. Zieber was dumbfounded; his old friend had betrayed him. His legs went and he dropped to a seat. He sat silent for a while, then stood and left without saying a word.

He went to confront Edward Clark, but Clark was in no mood to negotiate. He had just time to put on his wig as Zieber rushed into his office. All Clark was able to agree was that Zieber had no written agreement and the best thing that he could do was sell out while an offer was on the table. After all Clark had already helped to remove Ransom and Phelps. He informed Zieber that no formal agreement ever existed over Zieber's share of the company and Isaac could transfer the patent to whoever he liked as no court would uphold a non-binding agreement on a patent before it was actually issued. Iffy, but certainly arguable in court.

Zieber finally understood that both Clark and Singer were in the same boat and had been undermining him at every opportunity. It was a harsh blow for George.

So the final partner was under attack. Isaac Singer used the same tactics that he had used on Ransom and so successfully on Phelps (he had constantly overworked and bullied old man Phelps until Phelps cracked and was bought out). There was just one remaining partner to deal with, and Clark was on the case.

Edward Clark had grown up in the manufacturing trade, as his father Nathan Clark was a successful manufacturer, so Edward could really get to grips, not only with Isaac's patents, but his manufacturing ideas as well.

Both men profited considerably from 1851 up until 1868 with the I M Singer Company partnership. It is actually possible to say that if it was not for Edward Clark, Singer's may never have grown to the amazing worldwide success that it eventually did.

However, George Zieber was still hanging on like a terrier. He was terribly overworked and in failing health but stubborn to the end. His health was probably due to the pressure Isaac Singer was putting him under to produce machines, as demand grew so rapidly.

Zieber made sure that he did not put a foot wrong, giving Isaac no chance to remove him. By August of 1851 business was booming with over $20,000 of orders and then the patent was finally granted.

Chapter 18

Zieber is Removed

Publications, delighted with Singer's amazing invention, announced that Clark and Singer equally owned the patent rights. Zieber was stricken with rage when he saw this; it was the final straw that broke the camel's back. The constant pressure finally made Zieber collapse and he was taken to his bed.

Isaac then made his move.

The legend goes that Clark went to see Zieber first to see how bad he was and report back to Singer. Isaac Singer, ever the dramatist, rushed to Zieber's bedside in the first light and with his friendliest acting face on. Isaac was shocked to hear that Zieber was dying. Zieber was even more shocked as it was the first that he had heard of this! When Zieber calmed down, Isaac listened patiently to all of poor Zieber's problems and promised he would look after Zieber's family after his death. Isaac let slip that Zieber's doctor had told him that Zieber may die during the next few days, and also broke the news that nearly all production of sewing machines had suddenly been stopped for legal reasons. The business was failing fast, and may need more investment money to survive!

It was a cunning and devious plan, but Isaac had to strike while he had the chance, and once his last old partner was gone the business would all be his and Edward Clark's. All that Zieber had to do was sign over his part of the business to Isaac.

As Zieber hesitated, to sweeten the pot, Isaac Singer offered more and more until they came to the huge sum of $6,000 with which he could pay off his debts and leave something to his offspring.

It seemed too good to miss. If only Zieber could have seen the future! He was about to make the biggest mistake of his life. The very next morning Isaac produced the paperwork for Zieber to sign. Failing fast, with the last light dimming from his eyes, Zieber signed over all his rights to the Singer patent and fell exhausted into a fitful sleep. Isaac Singer promptly left with the most important piece of paper he was ever to hold. And so by March of 1852 Clark and Singer were sole owners of the Singer business.

It was no surprise when Zieber recovered! It turned out that Isaac had never spoken to Zieber's own doctor and had fabricated the 'dying' issue. In a stroke of devious genius, Isaac Singer had most of his business back and for what would become a mere pittance of the company's future wealth.

To make things worse for Zieber, (once fit and knowing he had been cheated, but now having some money), he shot across to

England to see if he could get ahead of Singer, but found the market and patents already sewn up. He reluctantly returned to America.

In a final twist of irony, Zieber, with no work, ended up working for Isaac as an employee, which he did for many years. He worked hard and even edited the I M Singer & Co Gazette, hoping that one day he would find himself on the generous side of Isaac and once again become a partner.

It never happened. Isaac kept Zieber close for a while until everything settled down and he was firmly established as the sole inventor of his sewing machine. He even invited Zieber around to his home and treated him like his old friend. Zieber was a clever man who had been beaten but kept his real feelings close to his chest. It pained him to see how well Isaac was doing; having grand pianos and plush furniture installed in his apartments, but by now there was absolutely nothing that he could do about it. Isaac had always implied that it was all Clark's fault but we all know that was not true.

Zieber openly disliked Clark, who he saw as the man who made it possible for Isaac to squeeze him out of the company partnership.

It is extraordinary to think that Isaac Singer could have been so cold blooded. Isaac Singer and George Zieber had been through so much together. When the pair had first met, according to Zieber, Isaac Singer hardly had a shirt on his back, his jacket was torn at the elbows and he had not eaten for days. Zieber had clothed and fed Isaac Singer and spent endless hours with him, talking of living the dream. Between them they had been through great hardships. Zieber had also borrowed heavily on his business and properties to invest in Isaac Singer's ideas, and helped him in countless ways.

Isaac Singer often showed his ruthless side where money was concerned. This was the side of Singer that many people felt when crossing the man that had grown up fast in a hard cold world.

Once Zieber had fully recovered he continued working for Isaac but it was a constant irritation to see Isaac's wealth grow, so when an opportunity arose in 1858 to get away from him, he took it. A new Singer branch office was being set up in Brazil – Zieber grabbed the chance and moved to Rio de Janeiro where he helped to set up Singer's South American agencies.

And so we say goodbye to Isaac's old friend and partner, the very man above all others who made it possible for Isaac to invent his sewing machine.

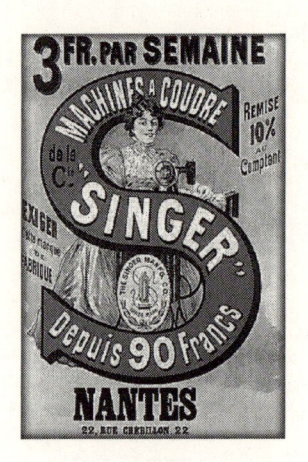

CHAPTER 19

Edward Clark firmly established his partnership and went on to become the financial genius behind the Singer name. There is absolutely no doubt that Edward Clark helped make Singers the powerhouse it became. Many historians tell that Edward and Isaac hated each other but that was far from the truth. As in all big business you have big personalities and both Clark and Singer were masters in their own fields, and although Clark and Singer were opposites they respected each other's abilities and together they were the perfect team. Clark also carried the fight to Elias Howe, and others, in court, all this for an equal lump of Isaac Singer's business.

In 1896 (published 1897) Singers produced a book on the history of the sewing machine, well their version of it anyway. I had been searching for a copy for nearly 10 years and finally managed to obtain one from a specialist bookstore in America. It was well worth the wait.

The book painted a bleak and incorrect picture of Elias Howe, stating that Howe had copied an earlier sewing machine made by Walter Hunt. At this point in history all the main instigators were dead so Singer's were unlikely to open a can of worms.

Singer's put it like this, "*In 1846 Elias Howe Jr built a sewing machine upon the Hunt plan, adding two puerile devices that were subsequently abandoned as useless, and procured a patent. Howe's machine was not, even in 1851, of practical utility. He had secured the patent on another man's ideas, planting himself squarely across any improvement, an obstructionist, not an inventor.*" Interestingly although the Singer book constantly praises Isaac Singer, there is hardly a mention of Edward Clark, simply referring to him as 'the best legal talent of that period'.

The book was so openly glowing of Isaac's effect on the world that it is hilarious; basically he single-handedly dragged women from the slavery of domestic work into the modern world. After a couple of pages I was starting to think, 'give me a break, he's going to walk on water any moment'. You think I'm kidding; here is an excerpt, "*for half a century it (the Singer sewing machine) has been a most potent factor in promoting the happiness of mankind all over the world.*" Oh, it gets worse. "*In its influence upon the home: in the countless hours it has added to women's leisure for rest and refinement; in the increase of time and opportunity for that early training of children, for the lack of which so many pitiful wrecks are strew along the shores of life*"... blah, blah, blah. Well that's enough of that. The book is so sickly sweet they must have soaked the pages in syrup before printing! Yes, the sewing machine was a brilliant invention but Singer's were pushing the boat out, maybe to collect all the wrecked children strewn along the shore!

Mahatma Ghandi was more concise when he simply said about

the sewing machine, *"One of the few useful things ever invented by man."*

Interestingly, Edward Clark had a hold over Isaac Singer that no one really understood. While Isaac could fly into spontaneous rages with almost anyone, with Clark he always backed down. We shall probably never know why he had this power or what knowledge he possessed that kept the raging Singer controlled. Maybe in the end it was simply that Edward Clark may have been the only real friend that Isaac ever had.

The partnership between Isaac Singer and Edward Clark turned out to be one of the most successful in sewing history and, although they probably did not trust each other, they became uneasy bedfellows in a global empire.

The Edward Clark Steamboat. People forget that Edward Clark also became amazingly wealthy and much of Singer's success came from Clark's business practices.

Chapter 20

Howe Beats Singer in Court!

Isaac Singer, with his persuasive manner, managed to get some of Elias Howe's sewing machine competitors to refuse to pay the huge licence fees that Howe was demanding.

In a rage Howe marched round to Isaacs and told him the demand for his patent had changed from $2,000 to $25,000 and if he did not pay he would regret it for the rest of his life (which turned out to be true). Isaac, who only a short period earlier had trouble raising $40, had no intention of paying Howe one red cent more than he was forced to. Once again a heated argument ensued and Howe was vigorously shown the door.

The stage was set for yet more legal wrangling and court cases. Eventually, even with all Clark's prowess, Elias Howe beat Singer in court, and Singer had to pay Howe huge sums. The biggest court case in American judicial history was coming to a head.

Luckily, by then Singer had the money to pay, so it was painful but no real hardship. If Isaac could have seen how much he would end up paying Howe, the $25,000 he had asked for earlier would have seemed like pocket money.

By the year 1853 Isaac was on a roll, and the Singer factory was now producing over 800 sewing machines a year. People say that this is not a lot but think about it for a moment. Isaac has set up a manufacturing plant with machinery that had to be made and modified for his machines from scratch. They had to go out and find companies willing to take the risk in these new-fangled machines and in 12 months they managed to bring in orders for over 800 machines. Pretty impressive, and with each factory giving them feedback the machine constantly improved.

They were still large sewing machines, aimed at the huge tailoring and garment industries in the cities. Isaac's first big sale was to a New Haven shirt manufacturer, where Isaac had shown his machine to be capable of sewing up shirts eight times faster than by hand. After extensive negotiation, something that Isaac was the master at, he walked away with an order for 30 machines.

The birth of the largest sewing machine company in the world was on a roll.

The success and huge expansion of the shirt company proved to all other businesses that they needed the humble sewing machine if they were to survive and compete in this new market.

Isaac used his achievements with the clothing manufacturers to place well-publicised advertising. His slow climb to success continued, but there was still one fly in his ointment – Elias Howe. Howe was blocking and suing Isaac and asking for more money each time they met.

Isaac decided to hire an even earlier sewing machine inventor, the respectable Walter Hunt, who claimed to have invented the sewing machine long before Elias Howe, and backed by Singer, Hunt applied for a patent upon his old sewing machine invention in an effort to destroy Howe's protection.

Isaac provided support and extra engineers to get Hunt's machine to court. Unfortunately for Isaac, the application was refused on the grounds of abandonment. This is fascinating reading…

Judge Charles Mason, Commissioner of Patents, May, 1854

"Hunt claims priority upon the ground that he invented the Sewing Machine previous to the invention of Howe. He proves that in 1834 or 1835 he contrived a machine by which he actually affected his purpose of sewing cloth with considerable success. Upon a careful consideration of the testimony, I am disposed to think that he had then carried his invention to the point of patentability. I understand from the evidence that Hunt actually made a working machine in 1834 or 1835. The papers in this case show that Howe obtained a patent for substantially this same invention in 1846.

Notwithstanding this, the Commissioner was forced to refuse Hunt's belated application, for the reason that an Act of Congress in 1839 had provided that inventors could not pursue their claims to priority in patents unless application was made within two years from the date when the first sale of the invention was made. Hunt had sold a machine in 1834, and had neglected to make application for his patent till 1853.

Thus it was that one of the grandest opportunities of the century was missed by the man who should rightfully have enjoyed it; the honours and emoluments of the great sewing machine invention passed to a man who neither had invented a single principle of action, nor applied a practical improvement to principles already recognized.

Judge Charles Mason then went on to attack Elias Howe…

Elias Howe, Jr., acquired the power, by simply patenting another man's invention, to obstruct every subsequent inventor, and finally to dictate the terms, which gave rise to the great Sewing Machine Combination about which the world has heard – and scolded – so much. Howe's machine was not, even in 1851, of practical utility. From 1846 to 1851 he had the field to himself, but the invention lay dormant in his hands. He held control of the cardinal principles upon which the coming machines must needs be built, and planted himself squarely across the path of improvement – an obstructionist, not an inventor – and when, in 1851, Isaac M. Singer perfected the improvements necessary to make Hunt's principles of real utility to the world Howe continued to obstruct and pursue litigation."

Walter Hunt testified, under oath, as follows…

"Elias Howe has several times stated to me that he was satisfied that I was the first inventor of the machine for sewing a seam by means of the eye-pointed needle, the shuttle and two threads, but said that it was irrelevant as he had the prior right to the invention because of my delay in applying for letters-patent."

So Walter Hunt, inventor of the safety pin and a repeating rifle, had claimed that he had invented a sewing machine, years before Howe. The story goes that it was Hunt's daughter that had actually put Hunt off patenting his invention, as she feared that thousands of women would find themselves out of work if he went ahead with making a sewing machine.

The facts turned out to be quite the opposite, creating a whole new industry and cheaper clothes for the masses.

While the court case was blustering on, one day Elias Howe spotted one of Isaac Singer's machines being demonstrated in a shop window and once again immediately went in to complain. Isaac was there and a furious argument ensued. Much to the amusement of the onlookers, the powerful Isaac booted Howe out of the shop.

Howe left flustered and angry. By now he was becoming wealthy from his royalty payments from other sewing machine manufacturers and was used to manipulating others, not being pushed around. He vowed Isaac Singer would pay dearly!

On the 4th of September 1854 tragedy struck the Singer family when Julia Ann Singer, who was just a few months old, died. She was buried in Greenwood Cemetery alongside Charles

Alexander Singer, (Isaac later named another of his daughters Julia Ann).

Isaac was at a terrible low in 1854; he had lost his daughter and lost in court to Elias Howe. Isaac was now being forced to cough up huge sums to his adversary and his business was faltering, the company not seeming to grow much past 800 machines a year. However 800 machines a year was still bringing in a vast amount of money which opened many doors for Isaac.

This is a rare woodcut of one of the very first factories to use sewing machines in 1854. This was the birth of true mass production in the clothing industry. The machines were driven by shafts connected to steam powered engines housed in a separate engine room. Only a few of the sewing girls were using machines the rest still hand sewing. It was back breaking work until better benches and chairs were invented for the machinists.

All the time the business was doing well, Isaac had taken the opportunity to move out of his humble apartment in Lower East Side. His old apartment held a lot of memories; it was where Mary Ann gave birth to his daughter, where he had worked on his sewing machine invention when he had no workshops and where his many children ran riot.

After moving to the house in East Fifth Street, as more sewing machine sales turned into money, they upgraded to a prestigious address at 374 Fourth Avenue, then up the road a jump to 395 Fourth Avenue.

And while his married life went on this way, Isaac continued to enjoy the additional company of many other women:

Mary Eastwood Walter, known as Mrs Merritt: She lived at 225 West Twenty-Seven St.
Mrs Judson worked at Singers in New York.
Ellen Brazee and Ellen Livingstone, both who may have borne him children.
Mary McGonigal, (sometimes spelt M'Gonigal) who was also known as Mrs Matthews, lived at 70 Christopher Street. I have named her children further down.
Mary Ann Sponsler, she had lived at 14 Third Avenue.
Also another young beauty, that appeared a little later on, was Kate McGonigal, younger sister of Mary McGonigal. I bet that caused a few rows!

Interestingly, there was a Mary McGonigal who was born around 1837 and went from Glasgow to America. Her parents were Hugh McGonigal and Sarah Coyle. It is a possibility that as a young woman she found work with her sister in one of Singer's premises, where she caught Isaac's ever-wandering eye.

Here are the eight surviving children (two died) by Mary Ann Sponsler, they were all named and left substantial wealth in Isaac's will, except for Violetta who, as we know, didn't receive a penny.

1837-1902, Isaac Augustus, Gus,
1840-1913, Violetta Theresa,
1843, John Albert,
Fanny Elizabeth,
Jasper Hamlet,
1848-1900, Mary Olive,
Julia Ann,
Caroline Virginia,

Now add four more kids with Mary McGonigal and two more with Mary Eastwood Walters (one died).

Mary McGonigal was known as Mrs Merritt in the Lower Manhattan area, where she lived with her daughter Alice, fathered by Isaac. Out of all Isaac's children, Alice was the love of Isaac's life and it broke his heart when he had to leave her behind. However, it all came right in Isaac's final days.

Don't forget the two original children, William and Lillian, with his only legitimate wife at this stage, Catherine Maria Haley.

Now I bet you have a thumping headache! Don't forget

mortality rates were terribly high at this period in history and several of the children from Isaac's every growing family sadly never made it to adult hood.

On a brighter note, do you get the impression that today Isaac could keep a sperm clinic going?

Amazingly Isaac managed to keep all of his families running. How was that possible? Well, he must have told his women that he travelled a lot, but as it turns out, he travelled just around the corner!

Chapter 21

Fight, Fight…

Let us get back to Isaac and his sewing machine court battles, for Elias Howe was not the only antagonist.

The legal battles rumbled on and on. Many years later Elias Howe allegedly tried to get Congress to allow him to extend, once again, his patent rights. Howe stated that the huge sums that he had made out of his patents was still not enough; needless to say popular opinion was not the same. He was slaughtered in the periodicals of the day and lost his extra patent extension.

Later Howe hired writers to boost his colourful version of the sewing machine saga, as did Singer's. I have a soft spot for Elias, the genius, so I won't say any more. You will have to read his amazing story that I am just finishing off, on the life of Elias Howe.

Isaac Singer was super-busy between 1851 and 1856, partly in court, partly in his new business, partly with women, but also designing ways to get around the main patents held by the great sewing machine kings, Howe, Wheeler & Wilson, Grover & Baker, Willcox & Gibbs and so on. Isaac Singer used all his talent and cunning to avoid Howe's costs while producing his sewing machines.

By 1855, against Isaac's initial wishes, Singers were expanding globally. Isaac was convinced that the company should expand in America first before conquering the world, but Clark was set on global expansion and would not be turned. It was his insistence on this that saved the company when the recession hit harder and harder at home. Monies coming in from abroad saved the company's bacon. By 1855 they had opened an agency in Paris and were setting up manufacturing there.

The recession sweeping its way across America made money much harder to borrow, and under the strain of constant expansion the business nearly collapsed under its continuing set-up and production costs.

However two people came to the company's aid in their lowest point. One was Edward Clark's father, Nathan Clark and the other was George Ross McKenzie.

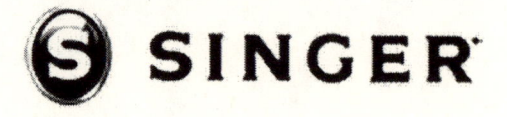

CHAPTER 22

GEORGE ROSS MCKENZIE
1820-1892

George Ross McKenzie was originally from Inverness, and started work for Isaac Singer in 1852. Initially he helped on the shop floor making cases for the sewing machines before he moved on to working on the new models. McKenzie was a man on the move and he shot up through the Singer company, expanding with it. Although George was only a worker, when he found out that the Singer Company was in big trouble he rushed out and raised $5,000. Not only did he invest this in Singer's business he talked the workers into taking a pay cut until the financial situation improved. George Ross McKenzie was instrumental in saving Singer's at its lowest point.

In 1858, Clark sent McKenzie over to Britain to build the largest sewing machine factory the world had ever seen, at Kilbowie, Clydebank, Scotland. They kept out of England because Elias Howe had sold his patent rights to a London manufacturer a few years earlier. William Thomas held Elias's all-important patents and would have charged Singer's for every machine they produced in England, however over the border in Scotland they were free to operate.

Eventually McKenzie became so important, he steered the company through some of its hard, early transitional periods. George Ross McKenzie eventually became president of Singers and a powerful man in his own right.

McKenzie continued to work successfully within the Singer Company for many years. He died a multi-millionaire and his will was read at Monticello because of the closeness of his magnificent country estate, called Glen Spey, at Lumberland, Sullivan County, New York.

When McKenzie died he had failed to update his will and left some of his estate to his wife, Rebecca (though she died two years before him) and his 12 children. He is buried in Glen Spey Cemetery, NY.

Chapter 23

So here we are in 1855. Even with the recession, the Singer Company was nearly out of the woods and Isaac, ever the optimist arranged a grand Christmas ball for his staff and other influential associates.

Meanwhile, Singer and Clark could still not get around the stumbling block of the large cost of their machines. Clarke had been busily opening agencies around the country and studying all information on the market and suggestions of how this could be solved.

Originally Singer sewing machines came onto the market at an astounding $300 each, a fantastic and impossible sum for most normal families. Elias Howe had worse trouble trying to sell his machine for $500. The average wage was less than $10 a week, so the machines were well out of the reach of everyone except the factories. However, with the increase in production the prices soon dropped to $125 and then lower still.

Isaac interviewed and employed countless beautiful women to demonstrate his sewing machines in shop windows, halls and auditoriums. His plans worked so well that the crowds often blocked the carriages from trying to move along the streets, and police were paid to keep traffic flowing.

Even with all the production problems and a North American recession, by 1855 Singer's dominated the sewing industry, selling 883 sewing machines in twelve months and took its first baby steps to becoming the largest sewing machine company in the world. However, the Singer machines were still way above what the man in the street could afford.

Now we are going to discover how our two capitalists made Singer a household name.

CHAPTER 24

THE FIRST HIRE PURCHASE SCHEME

Who remembers the Tallyman, or 'knocker'? I do; when I was a kid it was the Providence man who came to our area. He would turn up once a week or at the end of the month to get his payments on borrowed money. He would lend money on 'easy terms' for Tommy's new shoes or a bicycle for the hubby, a little extra at Christmas.

A million *Tallymen* kept their books of payments and travelled around the poorer communities of the world. Items were bought on 'the never never' (because you never owned them or finished paying for them) and some poorer estates even had the nickname of *Neverland*, because of the constant money lending where most things were bought on '*Tick*'.

This system was so popular that Clark identified a way to really earn his share of the Singer business. Not only did he keep the opposition's lawyers tied up in court, but also with his excellent staff, he devised the first official hire purchase or instalment plan in America. It was the ideal scheme for Singer's expensive sewing machines. Isaac was reluctant at first but after a successful trial run and a boost in sales directly attributed to the instalment plan, Isaac was soon converted and gave it his full support.

As we know, Isaac's latest sewing machine was being marketed for $125, less for cash. Isaac had managed to cut his manufacturing costs but still could not get a machine within reach of the masses. Every day people who could not afford the $125 for a Singer machine but could pay a small amount per week or month managed to take home a sewing machine, and so the Singer never-never was born.

Clark offered a Singer for the unbelievable sum of just $3 a month, payable over several years until the machine was paid for. Suddenly, fully guaranteed, brand new Singer sewing machines were available to everybody.

Clark also devised multiple or group purchases where several people could get together to buy one machine or more. Families could pay together, or schools, work colleagues, streets of neighbours, even church clubs could all buy a sewing machine together. Also Singer's now offered a trade-in plan against the customer's useless old sewing machine. These machines were immediately destroyed and the raw materials recycled into new Singers, a practice the company continued right up until the 1970's.

Clark's hire-purchase scheme, that seems so obvious and simple today, was revolutionary and brilliant in its time. Of course hundreds of years before Clark, even in the Bible, there had been bartering and exchange, money lending and part-payment, but it was Clark who really did the paperwork and made it part of our everyday life with an officially recorded, documented and enforced payment scheme that could be rolled out anywhere in the world.

Today everything from sofas to our cars can be bought on schemes originating from Edward Clark back in 1856.

This totally revolutionary practice changed not only America, but also our planet. The sudden ability for the average man in the street to afford previously unaffordable things changed everything. A rapid industrial boom was on its way and the American economy flourished.

This is a genuine British Singer hire purchase slip, one page from a whole book of them. Each page would have the amount paid weekly or monthly cut off the top. Amounts were changeable from one shilling to one pound depending on your circumstances. Each week the customer would take the hire-purchase book to their local Singer shop where the amount paid would be filled in, signed and dated by Singer's staff.

By creating the first publicly accepted hire purchase scheme in the world, Edward Clark and Isaac Singer, the ultimate capitalists, had pushed our world into the modern era.

Let us look at a more recent example. The average payment in 1936 for a standard hire-purchase agreement with the Singer Company (in England) was two shillings and six pence a week (half-a-crown). The average woman's wage was little over one pound a week. A Singer model 28k, which retailed for around £30 would have been paid for over several years, (with one pound being 20 shillings).

This meant a customer would pay weekly over roughly 240 weeks for their sewing machine. I once met a customer who paid for their machine at the lowest payment for 15 years, from 1926 to 1941 – inconceivable today! You can see that the price of a sewing machine would relate more to a price of a car today, expensive or what!

So that is how our two businessmen managed to market and sell their expensive products back in 1856.

Also, 1856 was the year that Singer's presented their first small domestic machine nicknamed the 'turtleback'. It was a bit of a disaster but it paved the way for much better domestic machines, which would soon flood onto the market, now split between domestic and the factories.

All this catapulted the Singer Company into the big time; sales went up from 883 in 1855 to a massive 2,564 in 1856.

Chapter 25

1857

At this point in history the courts had finally established beyond any doubt that just a handful of men held all the important patent rights for sewing machines.

Over the years, as the cases continued, patent offices around the world were searched. It proved that these few 'sewing machine kings' held immense power – if only they could just stop arguing with each other!

Orlando B Potter, president of the Grover & Baker sewing machine company managed to get all the men around the table for reconciliation talks; he had a cunning plan. The sewing machine kings settled down to smoke peace pipes. After years in court, and the largest mountain of legal documents in American judicial history, they finally gave up suing each other.

All the patent holders pooled their patents and formed *The Sewing Machine Cartel*. Edward Clark drafted the papers and for the first time in history, patent pooling happened in 1857.

I can just imagine the tension in the room when they all met. These powerful men had been attacking each other for years, but the chance of huge benefits made them nervous bedfellows. What they were planning was really an illegal monopoly and many years later their cartel needed government legislation to crush it.

The all-powerful *Sewing Machine Cartel* spent years suing all other fledgling sewing machine companies. This allowed 'the powerful few' to dominate sewing machine production and become rich, stifling much of their American competition. See what I mean about them being ruthless capitalists! And what will make you laugh is that all the while Isaac is agreeing with the Cartel, in 1857 he patented 12 new ideas, which he only shared with his partner Clark, and certainly with none of the other members. So he was talking one way with the Cartel and going another, quietly behind their backs.

Eventually, as all the patents ran out the Cartel was destroyed, and its demise ushered in a new era of affordable sewing machines for the masses. Sewing machine patent applications went from the first proper sewing machine patent, by John J. Greenough in 1842, to a handful between the 1840's and 1850's to hundreds, then to thousands and tens-of-thousands. In a few years the great sewing machine pioneers would fade into history.

Isaac Singer made a box for transporting his sewing machine. The box then converted into a sewing platform which the operator could use as a treadle.

Chapter 26

Once again we are jumping ahead. Let's get back to Isaac Singer, for he still has a long journey ahead of him and plenty of excitement, including two wars.

Out of all of Isaac's original patents, he missed a big one. He failed to notice that the treadle cabinet that he made to store his machine in, and on which it was used, was unique. He was beaten to the patent office and missed out on patenting the treadle base of his own machine! Oh, how that must have stung our eager capitalist.

So why buy one of these new-fangled sewing machines? None of them had ever worked properly before. Why buy a Singer? Who was Isaac Singer? Certainly not the household name he is today.

The answer to this is hard work. Isaac figured out that he needed to spend a minimum of 10,000 hours promoting his product to get it off the ground, so he hit the road with his machine. This magic number is still used by agencies today with new products, from unknown pop bands to vacuum cleaners.

With Clark watching his back on the legal side, it was time for the showman to return. This is where Isaac Singer's superb salesmanship came into action. Much like before, in his acting career he packed up his machine (in the case he had forgotten to patent) and he and his entourage rolled out of town. Isaac went to shows, to theatres, to factories, playhouses and church gatherings – "Gather round ladies and gentlemen, come and see the future! The miracle of modern engineering is here. My machine will release women from the drudgery of daily work."

He tirelessly demonstrated his amazing invention that not only stitched well but was also guaranteed to stitch for 12 months without failure.

All of his acting skills started to pay off, as he used them to promote his machine. The master showman also had a great publicity stunt up his sleeve.

Isaac went to one of the largest sewing factories in America with the press in tow. Remember, up until this point in history every single item of clothing was made by hand. At the factory his sewing girl (probably another mistress) was going to race with not one – or two – but three of the fastest hand-sewing girls in a factory of over 3, 000 staff.

He unpacked his sewing machine, the official timekeeper made sure the girls were ready and then dropped his hand and off they went. By the end of the race not only had Isaac's girl beaten all three hand-sewing girls, the machine had worked flawlessly, and with the much stronger two-thread lockstitch, rather than their single threads hand-stitch.

The press were impressed; the factory was too, placing an immediate order for the machines (though some say sneaky Isaac had arranged the factory order with the owner beforehand).

Isaac even set up a large outdoor demonstration just along the road from the famous P T Barnum. More people flocked to Singer's demonstration than to Barnum's museum on Broadway!

Isaac Singer, after struggling for most of his life had finally come of age, and so had the sewing machine. Almost single-handedly, with bloody determination and against all the odds, Isaac Singer had ushered in the dawn of the sewing machine industry.

CHAPTER 27

MASS PRODUCTION

After the initial 'new-business' difficulties (until 1855 when the company kept borrowing to survive), Singer machines started to sell at an amazing rate. For the first time in history, proper mass production was thriving and new businesses were popping up like mushrooms on a wet autumn evening. The new age had arrived, which affected not only sewing machines but also more deadly inventions such as firearms.

It is said that several gun manufacturers that had pioneered some of the earliest mass production techniques, gained improvements for their arms production from the sewing machine industry, touring Isaac's amazing state-of-the-art factory in Mott Street, New York.

At this global centre of innovation and manufacturing they picked up tips on how to mass duplicate high quality parts with ultra-modern machinery. Remember sewing machines had to be perfect; the thickness of a single strand of hair was the difference between a machine sewing and not sewing. The tolerances Singer's were working with were even higher than the watch making industry. The factory, which opened in 1857 could knock out over 1200 complete and perfect sewing machines every single month.

This picture, courtesy of Singer's is from 1896. Shortly after this picture they started building the first skyscraper in the world behind the building, which was completed in 1906. By that time Singer's were making over 1,000,000 machines a year and supplying around 80 percent of the world's sewing machines.

The Mott Street factory, smack bang in the middle of New York, cost over $300,000 to build and equip. It was set on eight floors and was the most modern manufacturing factory in the world. It also had beautiful offices and in the showroom it had amazing white marble pillars and walnut tables. Office staff told customers that it was like going to work in a palace.

Unlike the secretive arms industry that kept their techniques under wraps, Isaac was openly boastful of his pioneering techniques and provided tours of his premises.

Singer's showrooms were impressive and women were shown how they could join two pieces of fabric. Back in the 1850's this was cutting edge technology.

Besides the *Singer Gazette*, dozens of periodicals toured and described in detail the amazing fireproof factory. Because of this open publicity, many firms benefited from the modern miracle of mass production and, we benefitted from lower prices in the stores.

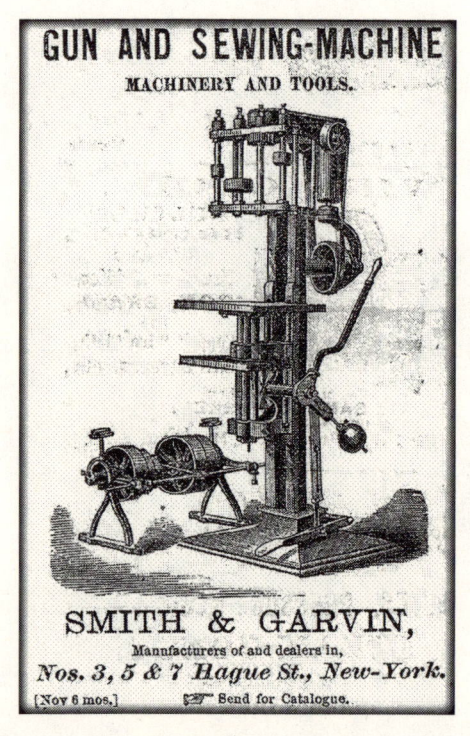

GUN AND SEWING-MACHINE
MACHINERY AND TOOLS.

SMITH & GARVIN,
Manufacturers of and dealers in,
Nos. 3, 5 & 7 Hague St., New-York.
[Nov 6 mos.]   Send for Catalogue.

From the 1850's American mass production was really on a roll and firms sprung up almost daily using techniques copied from Isaac Singer and the sewing machine trade.

As word spread about the reliability of Singer's machines, money started rolling in for Isaac, and sales were moving faster and faster.

Chapter 28

By 1857 I M Singer & Co had survived all their start up and manufacturing problems and even a North American

A rare woodcut of men decorating the Singer New Family sewing Machine. The machine was painstakingly finished by hand in gold.

depression. The company was booming, making over 3,600 machines a year.

This point in history is now long forgotten, but 1857 was the very start of mass production around the world for the clothing manufacturing industry, which then spread to just about every other industry as well.

Countless other industries also benefitted from the sewing industry, including some unlikely ones such as whalers. I know it seems weird, but let me explain. Whalers hunted whales for the oil, which burnt with a cleaner flame than kerosene. Also the oil from the sperm whale was perfect for oiling sewing machines. Then there were the glassmakers who would make the glass for the oil bottles, and the couriers from the steam ships to the railways. In a million different ways, from forklifts to fabric, the humble sewing machine changed our world. Within a few decades, there would be over 300 factories making sewing machines in Germany alone.

Edward Clark's clever hire purchase plan had helped tremendously and was copied by all the other sewing-machine makers of the day, and then by just about every major manufacturing and selling company in the world.

Clark also instigated a trade-in system, where customers swapped old machines for new ones at a ridiculously high rate of $50 per trade. All old machines were quickly destroyed to stop them being resold.

This policy continued right up to the 1970's and many Singer shops had presses in their storerooms to crush old machines. I know for sure that the Singer shop in Eastbourne, my hometown, had a seven-ton press in the basement for crushing competitor's machines.

At last, Isaac Singer's machine, which he had *invented-copied-made-improved*, was to revolutionise the world and provide him with untold wealth until his death. He had become the first capitalist, long before the likes of Bill Gates.

His bank balance, along with is waistline expanded rapidly.

Chapter 29

1859

Isaac Singer was a flamboyant and good-looking man at his peak – and now had money rolling in beyond his wildest dreams. He let Clark run most of the daily grind of their business while he set about enjoying the fruits of his labour. Remember, this was a man who had run away as a child, nearly died of starvation and was now on his way to a fortune. He was the American dream on two legs.

He moved the family on mass with Mary Ann to an imposing property at 14 Fifth Avenue full of staff. He employed tutors for the children and a full time doctor, Bill Maxwell, to look after them all. Eight coaches were kept along with around a dozen horses and coachmen. He had one specially made racing carriage, based on the old Roman races, which was pulled by five horses and capable of high-speed travel through New York. Isaac was full of bluff and bluster, which was just what the virgin sewing machine company needed. He was up against stiff opposition and he needed to show that Singer's were the number one sewing machine to buy.

Isaac had great parties at his offices and rented ballrooms in New York. He would dress up and swan around with a collection of his children around him. He always referred to any of his children as Singer. Whoever the mother was, he would introduce the children as Alice Singer or William Singer and so on. To him they were all his, and he was Isaac Singer. He had the grandest and most expensive parties, loved dancing and telling tales of his early struggles and hardship, as well of course, as his genius.

All his workforce and agency staff members were well cared for, and were offered Singer machines at a cut rate price in attempt to make them walking adverts for the brand, exploding with enthusiasm for Singer's at every opportunity.

His office parties became renowned and as sales grew his advertising became more and more boastful. All this drove his competitors mad as they tried to play catch-up. Today, Singer's is the single original sewing machine manufacturer to survive. His company, his sales techniques and his dogged persistence founded the only sewing machine 'name' that has made it from 1851 to the present day.

Chapter 30

Isaac now did everything in flamboyant style. He was a trendsetter. He often travelled to work in a specially commissioned coach or 'sociable', which was the finest ever seen in America. He designed and patented it, Patent No 25920. It was bright yellow, over 30 feet long, had toilets, a bar, cloakroom, smoking room, nursery, beds, seating outside for 16 and space for luggage for at least a dozen people. The monster had a special carriage home built for it behind his apartments and was pulled by matching black horses, six of them three abreast, costing a $1,000 each!

Isaac had always appreciated good horses from his years on the road but now he indulged in fine bloodstock, a hobby he carried through his life and his children continued.

The *New York Times* called his huge 3,800-pound coach a steamboat on wheels.

He would ride through Central Park to his magnificent office and everyone would know who was coming. Children would often run alongside his carriage, shouting to him in the hope of a few coins. He had special coachmen to keep them off.

Actually I was told that amongst his fine carriages and five-team racing carriages, he also had an insignificant little black cab that he kept quietly at work for his sneaky outings to various females.

Chapter 31

1860

By the early 1860's, Isaac was now the father of at least 18 children (that we know about!) and the main Singer factory, in Mott Street, had produced over 20,000 machines.

The beginning of the American Civil War was crippling for some industries and a boom for others. Both Isaac and Edward Clark were staunch Union men but many of their agents, suppliers and workforce were not, so they kept as quiet as possible where it affected the business. While the war raged sewing machines were shipped to every corner of North America on wagons, boats and the ever-growing railways.

Singer's sneakily managed to get over a thousand sewing machines and accessories to Grant's army by using the excuse that they were surplus stock, and after the war they openly used that donation of machines in their advertising.

Edward Clark was kept busy, this time in the Baltimore courts, where someone called Walmsley, had decided to claim that Isaac should never have been allowed any of his original patents. It turned out that he was secretly backed by an unhappy Phelps, who was now claiming that it was he who had done most of the work on the original Singer machine, along with an engineer named Mr Lafetra.

It all came out in court, that Phelps was the man behind the action. While all this was going on, and the court case continued, Isaac rented a suite of rooms at the Barnum's Hotel and spent two months in style and comfort with Mary Ann.

Singer's Baltimore lawyer, Latrobe, was well versed by Clark and as the case dragged on, Clark somehow managed to switch the most important witness, Lafetra, to his side (probably paid off) and won the case.

After the case concluded, a furious Isaac gave Phelps a piece of his mind and a final warning to back off. The two never spoke again.

While the trial was rumbling on, Clark came to Isaac with the final divorce papers from Isaac's first wife. After 30 years of marriage, Isaac's divorce came through for Catherine, amazingly on grounds of her on-going adultery with a Mr S Kent!

This sounds so implausible, until we find that Clark offered Catherine $10,000 to agree to adultery. It was a take it or leave it offer on the table for the shortest of time because, as Clark earnestly protested, the Singer Company was failing fast and if she didn't take the money it may be too late.

Isn't it funny how every time the two partners are paying someone off, their company is on a down turn and yet Singer is prancing around like a Roman emperor?

Clark was obviously hoping that Isaac would then be able to quietly marry Mary Ann and make all his New York society children more acceptable. He thought that if it were handled quietly out of the area then no one would ever know that they had not been married all along, but Isaac had other ideas.

Isaac was on a roll; he was a free man and much to Mary Ann's surprise he refused to marry her. Isaac could now attach himself to whomever he wanted and his eyes were firmly fixed on his lover, Mary McGonigal.

This is the point at which his lover of 25 years becomes his greatest adversary. Mary Ann must have been quietly devastated and her love turned slowly to scorn. Isaac's inability to love one woman was going to haunt him and his character for eternity, for Mary Ann would become his biographer and public executioner in the media and paint a false picture of a tyrant. Had Isaac any inkling of what Mary Ann was capable of, or what she was going to do, he would have probably been much more careful in his handling of the mother of eight of his children.

Isaac was oblivious and it seemed that he could not spend his wealth as fast as he was earning it. To Isaac it must have seemed like he was the owner of the best oil well in Texas, and that it just poured out wealth on a daily basis.

Within decades Singer's dominated world production,

producing two out of every three sewing machines made anywhere on the planet. By 1900 the company was making over a million machines a year and Isaac's estate would be getting a cut.

> *A more dissolute man never lived in a civilized country.*
> *He is in the constant habit of seducing females*
> *who submit to his base desires.*
> *Mary Ann Sponsler*

Ignoring Mary Ann's gestations, Isaac Singer went on to embrace the good life. He had a string of mistresses and managed his affairs with little privacy, giving the papers of the day wonderful print material. Poor old Clark – anticipating that securing the divorce with Catherine would calm the waters, he had actually freed the monster from his cage. As Isaac's wealth grew, so did his excesses.

We have often seen this before, where a person becomes incredibly wealthy but has no guiding force from parents and siblings. They seem to have no guidelines, no rules and they make a million sociably unacceptable errors. So many times they seem to burn in the fire of their own celebrity.

Isaac's offspring rose in number, almost by the month. Rumours persist that he had at least 35 children, possibly more, by a dozen or more wives, mistresses and lovers. There were probably some children that he did not even know he had!

However, although often publicly portrayed as a bigamist, as far as I can prove Isaac was only ever legitimately married twice and not at the same time.

Chapter 32

Now we need a break from our wandering-eyed capitalist, so let's have a look at his machines.

There were not many Singer sewing machine models that Isaac was involved with, but here are a few.

- **1851.** **Singer No1.**
- **1854.** **Singer No2.**
- **1856.** **Singer No3 Heavy duty.**
  Singer models 4-9 assorted variations of the above.
- **1856.** **Singer original Family, nicknamed the grasshopper or Turtleback, a failure that led to a superb machine.**
- **1859.** **Singer Letter A, Singer's first really popular machine.**
- **1863.** **Singer New Family, which evolved into the Singer 12, the finest and bestselling sewing machine in the world for many years.**

Chapter 33

Isaac's Arrest

By this point in Isaac's life, the press were describing him as the 'great sewing machine magnate'. He was still up to no good however, and this time with the paparazzi on his trail and a dedicated ex, Mary Ann, trying to trap and destroy him. How he managed to keep his intriguing life going is anybody's guess! He was burning the candle at both ends and apparently loving it!

Isaac's excesses had to come crashing down, and it happened spectacularly in the summer of 1860.

An incident occurred that caused uproar and ended with Isaac being arrested. I have always wondered if this was not an elaborate trap sprung by Mary Ann.

On 7 August 1860 Mary Ann was in her carriage driving along Fifth Avenue when she passed, supposedly by accident, a brand new French 'Diligence' closed carriage. Curiously she glanced inside only to see Isaac with his mistress, Mary McGonigal (who he had interviewed and hired to work for him at his

Philadelphia offices).

Mary Ann chased the carriage and forced it to stop, at which point a huge row then erupted in the street. Mary Ann later denied that she used any particular language, stating that she just kept screaming at Isaac until he fled.

When Mary Ann went back to her home, Isaac was waiting for her. This public outburst was not to be tolerated. However, Mary Ann, who was the injured party, flew into another rage. Isaac again became furious, a huge fight broke out and neighbours fetched the police.

Mary Ann said it was a brutal and bloody assault, in which he had knocked both Mary Ann and their daughter Violetta unconscious. The papers had a field day.

I M Singer,
The great sewing machine magnate, of 14 Fifth Avenue was arrested on complaint of assault and put under bond of peace for six months.

Isaac was in a bad situation and to make peace, promised to marry Mary Ann as soon as he could, but she was having none of it. She had now gone past the point of no return and the only benefit she would have from Singer would be a financial one. She had been the woman scorned and she aimed all her fury at bringing Isaac down.

Now remember that Mary Ann was a trained and skilful actress, and she used all her might to appear to the public as the wronged woman.

Although she never married Isaac legally, she sued him for divorce. Good one eh! Her idea was that because she was the mother of his children and they had lived together for so long she could legally divorce him as his common-law wife and claim a huge settlement. She approached Abbott & Fuller Associates and put her case to them – even if it was a weak one, Isaac now had deep pockets and would probably settle a fair sum on Mary Ann.

Mary Ann's case went to court in December of 1861. Along with her lawyer Fuller, she used all her skills to paint an awful picture of Isaac. In her public tales she relives how she was giving birth in their tiny apartment next to his partly-built invention, how she struggled for food while Isaac strolled around in comfort.

This is where, once again the line blurs. If we are to believe half of what she said in court, Isaac was a brutal and dangerous man.

This is just not the case; even old business partners and colleagues objected to her portrayal, and for every one person who Mary Ann found to scold Isaac, there was 20 who praised him.

Mary Ann was a cunning and deeply motivated woman, but a proven liar as well. Today she would have been lucky to get away with what she said in court without legal repercussions.

Mary Ann also thought nothing of changing the rules to suit her. For some time she had been having a fling with John Foster, a railway agent, and a few months later on 12 June 1862, she quietly crept away and married him. On the form she put her age down as 31, when in fact she was 45 at the time with eight children! John must have known about the children and presumably managed to do the math, so we guess he was just totally smitten.

However in court she was flawless. I mean Isaac had even been arrested for the assault on her! Now alarm bells started to ring with Isaac and he realised that he may have been set up in a long game.

Mary Ann needed proof of his infidelity and a weapon to use against him. Did she go to the park that day to trap him all along? Was she secretly following him trying to catch him with other women? Did she purposely enrage Isaac so that she could have the police called? Were all these plans put in motion that day back at Bertram's Hotel when the divorce papers came through from Catherine and Isaac told Mary Ann that he would never marry her? Had he unleashed a bitter enemy who would haunt him until his dying days? The answer to all these questions was YES.

In court Mary Ann had amassed a huge amount of information, naming several of Isaac's mistresses. Isaac had to admit under oath that he was guilty of adultery. Poor old Clark must have hung his head in despair. At last Isaac's well-hidden trails were being publicly displayed and there was enough dirt to allow the court to swallow everything else Mary Ann threw in with it.

Mary Ann worked her magic on the judge, who swallowed her tales hook line and sinker, for although she and Isaac were never married, the judge ordered Mary Ann the highest divorce settlement ever awarded in American courts at the time – the huge sum of $8,000 a year. Oh, how Mary Ann must have swanned out of the courtroom that day, but her victory was short lived.

Isaac was down but not out. Before the courts could finalize the order, Isaac, Clark and McKenzie came up with an offer Mary Ann could not refuse. They offered her a plush new home in the city at 189 West Twenty-Eighth Street, and $200 a month plus financial support for the children. The house would remain hers until it passed to her children after her death.

She accepted these terms but then got herself into a pickle. If she was technically married to Isaac as the judge implied, then she was also a bigamist, as she had married John Foster. So Mary Ann quietly continued to secure her divorce papers so that she could become legitimate. Obviously it would not work; as soon as Isaac was informed she had to quickly drop the case before he became suspicious.

Undeterred, (you have to admire the woman) in April 1863, Mary Ann went to court once more on grounds of fraud as Isaac had not paid her all the dues that he had guaranteed, or sent over the deeds to her house. At this point Isaac was still paying for his children, but obviously not enough.

Mary Ann knew how precarious Isaac's position in the press was and thought she could apply some pressure. Now that he was a public figure, for the first time, she had power over him. However as the court proceeding came to a head, Isaac and Mary Ann had a quickly arranged meeting. After the meeting she left the room and instructed her lawyer to immediately drop the case.

I would love to know what Isaac offered, or threatened. It is possible he may have threatened to sue her for bigamy, which carried a jail sentence. He had found out about Mary Ann's marriage to Foster from one of his children and was certainly furious, as you can understand. She was suing him, saying she was his wife, but had slipped away and got hitched herself. Before Mary Ann left the office, Isaac forced her to sign a paper renouncing her former relationship between them as common law man and wife.

That did not stop Mary Ann; as we shall see she was just getting started. She was a ball of fury.

The lines between these two are so muddy it is hard to see clearly. We know that Mary Ann's husband, John Foster, was attacked one night near his home. After all the trouble he had caused for Singer, no one was quite sure who the culprit was. Incidentally, Mary Ann had only divulged the secret marriage to her daughter following an accident, when she feared she was dying and needed to organise her will.

Out of all the adversaries Isaac had, all his troublesome partners, mistresses and wives, Mary Ann stands out as the most determined and dogged. She was out to get what she wanted at all costs.

Chapter 34

Now let's go back a step into this twisted romantic web. Isaac was running several families and mistresses and was most deeply entwined with Mary McGonigal, with whom he had five children. I wonder if he smiled to himself having two Marys; he couldn't slip up with their names.

How did the man do it? Simply astounding. He now has at least

Singer's machine being advertised. This is possibly the only picture of Mary McGonigal, known as Mrs Matthews, who had worked at Isaac's Philadelphia offices before he brought her to New York to live at 70 Christopher Street.

17 children that we know of and there are more kids on the way – oh, and another Mary!

After Mary Ann's marriage to Foster came to light, Clark acted once more to try and finally pay her off. She bickered on, causing more and more trouble, but Isaac let Clark handle her and closed the door on that chapter of his life.

And so the final ties were cut with the woman who bore Isaac 10 children and had been with him for nearly 30 years. As far as Isaac was concerned, Mary Ann was out of his life forever, and when he ever mentioned 'that woman' he called her 'Mrs Foster'. But Mary Ann is not quite out of our story yet for, as we will find out, as she did come back to chase Isaac's ghost.

Many times he lived with his lovers and partners under assumed names such as Matthews and Merritt. He set up women in hotels and apartments, showering them with gifts. When I think of Isaac, I am always reminded of King Henry VIII, as they certainly had several shared traits.

How did he keep it all going? All this intrigue makes Isaac's real life almost impossible to follow, as he was a walking, talking secret, gushing lies faster than water from a leaky pipe. It is possible that specialists would tell us that he was over-compensating for his very hard start in life. Not only could Isaac now afford a new suit, he could buy the shop and the women in it!

Incidentally, although Singer's made special machinery for other companies, they never made sewing machines for anyone except for themselves. This was unlike most of the other companies, who were only too happy to put any name you wanted on the front of a machine if you bought enough of them. In the 1860's Isaac Singer was still busily improving his machines, and right up until 1867 he was submitting a stream of patents to the Patent Office.

Isaac was now at his peak and buzzing around 24 hours a day, not only with work but enjoying all the benefits of the massive wealth that just kept on growing.

Chapter 35

Of course it eventually all caught up with him – I mean it had to, didn't it! Isaac's constant womanising, a series of public scandals and numerous court cases had turned many Americans against him, and that in turn, hurt Singer sales. He had been scandalised in the papers and so became ostracised from society.

This seems to have been taken like water of a duck's back to our inventor. Remember, Isaac was the consummate showman and seemed to be blustering his way through the lot. It was as if he was playing a part in one of his plays, seducing each female in turn. I have no doubt that he loved many of his mistresses and wives. His ability to fall head-over-heels for someone and treat them like a queen was balanced by his darker side and black rages when things went wrong. With his exceptional love came the ghost from within.

There is an old adage that goes… *Success can help wash away sins of the past.* I think that Isaac was brilliant at washing away his past and most of his women went quietly on their way with a suitable pay off. However a few did not!

Periodicals say that Isaac Singer could be rude-mouthed, hot-tempered and arrogant. Some women obviously loved it, though in reality his dark side was his undoing. Clark constantly had to work around his partner and expand the company. At one point he had a loan for expansion denied by the bank on grounds of moral turpitude. How crazy is that!

There is also a conflicting story that in September of 1860 Isaac Singer escaped the country under an assumed name while on bonded release.

They say Clark helped Isaac to flee to Europe, and while he was keeping out of harm's way he could set up more agencies and promote Singer machines until the coast was clear. I don't know how true this is but I do know that once Isaac was out of the way Edward Clark could get back to running the company, rather than bribing Isaac's women to avoid the press and ever hungry public.

So our story continues with Isaac fleeing America on 19 September 1860; not with his last squeeze, Mary McGonigal, but with her 19 year old sister Kate! He's a slippery devil. The showman boarded under the assumed name of Mr Simmons (travelling with companion). They travelled aboard the famous Great Eastern on its return voyage to England and then by rail to London, lodging near his London offices in Cheapside.

Isaac was like a kid on summer holiday, with the bonus of being able to do whatever he liked. Once again his lack of early guidelines, control and morals came to the fore.

The Victorian London offices facing St Paul's Churchyard.

Isaac soon tired of Kate and packed her off. He then picked up a British beauty called Lucy; of whom I have unfortunately found out nothing other than she was sent to New York by Isaac, for a short period and was named by Mary Ann in her divorce papers.

Everywhere Isaac went he was a sensation. The rich American

was news. Clark forwarded Isaac money as he needed and the London banks were delighted to have his patronage. He travelled in style and spent money like water. For every cent he spent ten more were coming in.

Isaac was American royalty and acted the part, having bright tailored suits made in Savile Row and collecting fancy beaver skin hats and silk coats, all charged to the Singer Company. His tall, skinny frame had filled out over the last few years to become a large and impressive figure. Isaac did not dress to the fashion – he dressed to impress. His early years in the carnival and on the stage had brought out the actor in him.

Isaac Singer was a self-made man, a fascinating breed of American who had made his own path, who had dragged himself up from the muddy frontier streets by his own genius. Isaac had no help; no pot of gold was waiting by his cot provided by generations of previous family members.

When he passed a street seller or popped into a coffee house, the people serving knew he had come from nothing and thought, 'I could do that, I could be him'. He knew how to talk to people; he had that 'common touch'. There was no pomp and circumstance surrounding the big man, and although he had little time for fools, he got on well with every section of British society.

Isaac was a wonder in London. He would stroll down the city streets in all his glory, with his specially made silver and ebony walking stick, like someone from another world. When the average height in Victorian London was five foot five inches,

Isaac when in his hat and handmade-heeled shoes would have been over seven feet tall! People would stop and stare at the impressive sight. When he went to the theatre he was more of a sensation than the production he had come to see.

However about to enter our story is the fascinating, beautiful and calculating lover, Isabelle Eugenie Boyer.

CHAPTER 36

ISABELLE EUGENIE BOYER
PART 2

Now our tale will split once again, for history tells us two versions of what happened next. We do know that Isaac travelled to Paris to see how his agency over there was doing. In Paris he met up with William Proctor (who Isaac had sent over to help set up the French manufacturing of Singer sewing machines). William and Isaac were good friends having worked together on his printing machine at Taylor's business years before, and I am sure William would have shown Isaac a good time in Paris.

One version of our tale tells that Isaac had visited Paris earlier in his travels and come across an attractive English woman from Suffolk called Pamela Lockwood, who was married to Louis Noel Boyer who ran a pension or inn (some say Louis was a confectioner from South Africa). Louis Noel Boyer and his wife had a beautiful daughter, Isabelle, who was born at 13 Rue Monceau, Paris on 17 Dec 1841. Isabelle Eugenie Boyer was later to be described in periodicals of the day as the most beautiful woman in Europe. Unfortunately when she met Isaac she was already married to an American, one Mr Summerville. The tale tells that while staying at Boyer's Inn they fell madly in love with each other. Isabelle was besotted and Isaac had found the woman of his dreams, though she was the same age as some of his children! Isaac then supposedly persuaded Isabelle to free herself and wait for his return.

The other story is that they first met in America when she was travelling with her American husband on honeymoon. I am sure that in the future, with our modern miracle of the Internet and records coming on line almost by the second the actual series of events will reveal themselves. Either way Isabelle was only 19 when she managed to split from her husband.

She could have had little idea of the littered trail of women and children that Isaac had left behind him in America, so Isaac promised Isabelle the world if she would be his wife.

Pretending to be a married couple, Isaac and Isabelle went on a Grand Tour of the great cities of Europe, combining business with pleasure. Some legends say that they even travelled as far as St Petersburg where, many years later, the Singer Company set up their Russian headquarters.

On their tours they bought works of art and beautiful furniture, statues and ornaments. Isaac promised Isabelle that when he died she would have all the 'goodies' they bought together, and he actually kept his promise in his final will and testament.

They travelled like the aristocracy of old, purchasing and

partying as they went. All the goods they bought were shipped back to America for the grand house that Isaac was planning to build in New York.

Isaac went back to New York in 1861, as Clark needed him to finalise the last paperwork for their new company. Also this would give Isaac the chance to tie-up his affairs and sort out the problematic Mary Ann, as well as his other mistresses. Then the coast would be clear for when he returned with his new love.

He was soon pining for Isabelle and went back to Paris as quickly as he could. In New York they were all out to get him, but in Europe they all loved him. Isabelle and Isaac travelled Europe in style for almost two years.

As soon as Isaac had returned to his lover, he promised to marry her, and by late 1862 Isabelle was pregnant.

By 1862, sewing machines were on a roll and caused huge excitement wherever they were shown. Here at the International Exhibition in London, the crowd are trying to get a peek at this amazing invention.

Chapter 37

1863

There is no doubt that out of all the busy years Isaac had, 1863 topped the lot. In that year he sorted out not only his wives and lovers but his company as well.

All the time Isaac was travelling, he was also working, as was Clark in America. The Singer Company was now making profits not only from sewing machines but everything to do with them, as well from threads and needles to patent rights, cases and cabinets, sewing attachments and much, much more. All in all the two capitalists were booming. They had taken every opportunity and every advantage open to them and milked it to the brim.

As Isaac made his way back to New York he thought that the rough waters he had gone through there would have settled, and America would have long forgotten all about him. He brought his new love back and installed her in his plush Fifth Avenue home.

Unfortunately nothing could be further from the truth; former wives and mistresses were waiting for the golden goose to return, as were the paparazzi. Within the month, Isaac was once again splashed all over the papers.

By this point Isabelle was heavily pregnant, and although Isaac had some trouble reaching a final settlement with Catherine, he managed to deal with this. An eight-month pregnant Isabelle then toddled down the aisle of the protestant Episcopal church of St John the Evangelist in Waverly Place, New York, to marry the man of her dreams. It was a warm day on 13 June 1863, as Isabelle leant on Isaac's arm in front of Reverend Edwin Cook. Isaac and Isabelle then retired home where a special group of family and friends celebrated their happy union.

But Catherine soon reared her head again, not satisfied with her settlement of $10,000, she tried for more from the wealthy Isaac. Isaac was so close to sorting all his women out that he flew into another frustrated rage. He was so furious that he threatened all concerned, including his own son William, (who was still working for Isaac at the time).

William was so scared from the confrontation, it stayed with him all his life and the two never spoke again. I have found no record of Catherine succeeding with her case for more compensation.

On 25 July 1863, just over a month after the wedding, Isabelle gave birth to Adam Mortimer Singer.

Chapter 38

The Singer Manufacturing Company

Isaac, now 52, thought that he had finally managed to deal with his sordid past. He was officially married for the second time. He had paid off all his former women and was providing for his enormous offspring. He had plenty of money coming in, and when he felt in the mood, would occasionally add a few ideas to the sewing machines, but he needed to release big funds from his company if he was to build his dream home in New York.

His long, grand tours with Isabelle had filled his mind with ideas, and he wanted to build a home in New York that no one had seen the like of before.

He had tussled backwards and forwards with Clark over the business, but just before his wedding to Isabelle, he had finally got it all sorted.

On 1 April 1863, with annual sales now topping over 21,000 sewing machines, the Singer Manufacturing Company was formed with a capital of $500,000 divided into five thousand

$100 shares.

Isaac immediately sold some of his shares to staff and raised $25,000 spending money. Isaac and Clark also split the $400,000 of government bonds that they held. In July they agreed to hand all other assets of the original partnership to the new company.

Now these figures were immense, remember the weekly wage was around $10 for the average man in the street, so $400,000 was a king's ransom. Interestingly several of the Singer Company men did not take up the share offer. They must have kicked themselves until their dying days for the shares just went up and up, spilling profits and dividends like ripe fruit.

Isaac remained on the board of trustees, but from this point onward, his input into the company dwindled and his interest became more of a financial one. However I have seen handwritten letters from Isaac as late as 1868, where his is still actively involved in sewing machine design and applying for patents in England. Ever the capitalist, he finished one letter with the glorious words, "The fountain head has not yet dried."

Incidentally, in the same year Singer's opened their first German agency in Hamburg.

Now married to Isabelle and free from all former women Isaac carried on with his grand plan to build a castle where he would bring up his legitimate son and future children in style.

Adam Mortimer Singer, Isaac and Isabelle's first child together, claimed to his dying day, to be the first of Isaac's legitimate sons, and even had it engraved on his gravestone in Paignton. I expect a few of Isaac's other children, especially William would have strongly disagreed.

Chapter 39

The Castle

Isaac loved his semi-retired life and went ahead with building his dream home, inspired by his grand tours of Europe.

Isaac Singer never thought that his last residence in the United States would be the Castle he had built in granite in Yonker's, County, Westchester. Not to be confused with the castle that Singer Company president Frederick Bourne later built on Dark Island.

The Castle was Isaac's pride and joy, and he filled it with the art and statues that he bought on his tours with Isabelle. It was at home at the Castle, just weeks before Lincoln's assassination at Ford's Theatre in Washington, that Isabelle gave birth to Isaac's second child by her. Born on the 8 January 1865, she was christened Winnaretta Eugenie Singer, and was known to all as Winnie.

Winnie grew up as the next generation of Singer's, and quite in keeping with her father's behaviour, she later stunned and shocked Europe in equal amounts. We shall hear a little of her amazing story later.

Let us sum up how well our capitalist was doing. Isaac Singer had become the figurehead of a multi-national company that was expanding into every country. Singer machines were being carted across African deserts and up the Amazon, with new agents appearing in every town. In the larger towns there would be several agents and shops, all selling Singer machines.

Isaac Singer was a dreamer, and he dreamt big, and like all great entrepreneurs, he surrounded himself with the best men, including Edward Clark. As the American Civil War came to a shuddering close, Singer's were set up and ready. His manufacturing plants were employing new staff, fresh from the conflict, and expanding into the dust and rubble of the war. It was great men like Isaac Singer who pulled America up by its shirt sleeves, to become the greatest superpower in the world.

Within 30 years Singer's had built huge factories, exported

This is the great American Singer factory at Elizabethport New Jersey, where Singer machines poured off the production line 24 hours a day. They were then shipped by rail and boat around the world.

across the world, set up agencies and outlets, factories and shops and were directly employing over 70,000 workers, as well as all the paraphernalia that went with them, from steam boats to trains, lumber yards to wagons, including 8,000 horses!

The Singer Manufacturing Company had become a giant, the likes no one had seen before, and they did it all themselves. It was becoming an enormous multinational. They set up and opened shops rather than supply other retailers.

Part of the Singer Companies' success was their stunning ability to manufacture specific sewing machines for specific jobs, from hat making to shoe manufacture.

By 1896, they had opened over 4,500 company offices around the world; they opened offices and head offices, agencies and sub agencies in every far-flung outpost from Bombay to the Transvaal, with their executive head offices being on Broadway, New York. As Singer's quaintly put it, *"On every sea are floating the Singer machines, along every road pressed by the foot of man, from the snows of Canada to the pampas of Paraguay."*

Little credit is given to these great men today, our first capitalists, but if you wound the clock back to the birth of America's huge power, standing there in the smouldering ruins of a broken country would be the impressive figures of Isaac Merritt Singer and Edward Clark.

Chapter 40

Isaac and some of his children from his previous families, Isabelle and her children, all lived in Yonkers for about another year-and-a-half, but things were about to change forever, because by April of 1866, Isaac would be moving lock stock and barrel, to Paris, France.

Singer had underestimated the deep resentment that some of the New York society held him in. Isaac and Isabelle put on grand parties at the Castle in Yonkers, but they were shunned by the important families of the day, and at some events, less than half the people invited showed up for an evening of free entertainment and dining.

This had a deeply upsetting influence on Isaac and Isabelle, who tried their hardest to be accepted, but never were.

Isaac's possible treatment of his former women, and Mary Ann's public annihilation, had come back to bite him, and no matter what he tried, he was deemed to be an outcast from high society. I can imagine that more than a few of the former women in Isaac's life were also poisoning the pot at every opportunity.

This infuriated the big man, but there was nothing much he could do about it. Even in 1863, when he and Clark had supplied General Grant and the army of the North with free sewing machines during the Civil War, it did little to endear the man to his fellow New Yorkers. There is no more believable publicity than a woman scorned, and in Mary Ann they had the ideal Whirling Dervish, creating a stink that could be smelt all the way to Europe.

If the future President of America, General Grant did not publicly embrace Isaac, then who would? Though it is said that in private they got on famously. Grant needed industrialists, capitalists and manufacturers to rebuild his nation, and Isaac was all three! In respect, Isaac even named his third child with Isabelle, Washington Merritt Grant Singer (his birth was to cause quite a stir as we shall see).

The main problem is that all of 'his' problems were now public affairs. The papers of the day hounded Isaac, as he was great copy for them. For example, one of the hot gossip stories was that of Mary Ann Sponsler, which had backfired for Isaac.

Mary Ann Sponsler was doing her utmost to publicly destroy Isaac after being unceremoniously dumped by him.

Isaac and Edward Clark allegedly had to come up with an amazingly cunning plan to get her out of New York. Clark offered her a nice sum of money to vacate her city home for a few days and take their children on a vacation. While she was away, they tried to force her out of her New York home permanently, (allegedly in cahoots with her own lawyer who must have paid very well indeed). The trick failed and became public knowledge.

It was actions like this that led an exasperated Clark to find a final solution to his on-going problem. Clark was quietly running much of Singer's in the background while the new president of the company, Inslee Hopper, found his feet. Clark made Isaac agree to step down from active participation in the new company with the promise he would be kept close to all the action. In reality it was probably just another of Clark's clever ruses to get Isaac out of the way.

You have to remember that Isaac's greatest inventions were done and dusted. The Singer Company had teams of engineers designing and improving the new models, and Isaac was just in the way. When he would come up with an idea it was like a grenade going off in the research and development lab, and it just interfered with the company's own production.

New York and the whole of America were getting just too hot for Isaac. He had burnt so many of his bridges that the whole place must have seemed on fire.

Singer and Clark were still board members, but Isaac constantly embarrassed Clark. All his negative publicity had a hold over sales and share prices.

Some tales say that Clark came to Isaac with a deal that would allow him to semi-retire and spend his wealth. Edward Clark's wife, Caroline, was delighted and probably encouraged her husband, for she was deeply religious and apparently hated

Isaac Singer and what he had been up to. Legends say that she would not let him step inside her house!

Singer, Clark, and their legal teams fought a pitched battle over the company shares, worldwide agencies and its assets until at last both sides were satisfied. Luckily, Isaac had a great young lawyer that lived near him called David Hawley, and Hawley fought on his side. Isaac was well aware, as was Clark, that this was the deal that would settle the Singer business for good, and it was the last chance for both of them to grab a piece of the pie.

As the deal came to a head, Clark had an ace up his sleeve. He offered Isaac almost everything he wanted, including a cut of future profits from the company on one condition, that Isaac left America!

It was a ridiculous to ask such a thing, as Isabelle was heavily pregnant again, but in front of Isaac was a carrot of such proportions that he knew he must take it. Clark and his team held their breath as the huge man deliberated with his legal team.

Isaac played his part in the Singer Boardroom arguing for the best deal. It meant he had to pack and leave but it would secure his wealth and income for life. He would have a cut of the company and technical input on sewing machines if he so wished.

What Clark never knew, was that Isaac and Isabelle had already decided to leave, and Clark had played right into their hands, offering far more than they needed. Hawley had already wound

Wheel-feed systems were popular
until teeth-feed mechanisms caught on.

up most of Isaac's affairs and they were ready to go.

Their Castle in the suburbs had been a big mistake; it was way too quiet for the couple. Isaac was in his early 50's and Isabelle was hardly 22, so neither was ready for the quiet life. Isabelle never fitted in to New York society and had probably been urging Isaac to move for some time, also to get away from his huge brood of children, some who were her own age. At that time the children could pop up at any moment, taking Isaac away from her and their own family. We all know what it is like to have children around you; well stop for a moment and think what it would be like to have over 20 of your husband's kids around you!

Isaac was now independently wealthy for life. While Isaac had wasted a lot of his money on frivolous things, such as huge handmade coaches, he had also been investing in land and property and had become rich from the profits (he owned over 100 acres of land around Yonkers alone).

The paperwork was drawn up at Singer's, scrutinized by all parties and signed. Inslee Hopper, now an established and successful president of the company, stacked all the papers up and the deal was done. Isaac shook hands with the other members in the boardroom and walked out of the Singer New York offices, never to return.

Chapter 41

Isaac prepares to leave America

Isaac moved fast. He was a born travelling man and knew what to do. The house had already been rented out, and all the best items that Isabelle and Isaac loved had been boxed up ready for transporting. He wound up the last of his financial and domestic affairs in America and booked passage aboard the luxury liner and mail ship, the SS City of Washington, bound for Queenstown and Liverpool, England.

Although Isaac and Isabelle were not appreciated in America, they knew Europe loved them.

The obvious place for the family to head for was Paris, France, where Isabelle had lived and they had numerous contacts.

Was it a sad day in 1866 when Isaac Singer and his family set sail for Europe? He left behind his American dream as well as 18 known children, and looked to the future in a foreign land. I wonder, as he saw the coastline of his homeland slowly fading away, if he knew that he would be leaving America, and most of his other children forever? Did Mary Ann secretly shed a tear, or have a glass of champagne to celebrate?

Whatever the truth, there must have been huge emotions from all parties; children, business partners, wives and mistresses. As his ship disappeared over the horizon Isaac had managed, once again, to wipe his slate clean and was off to a new start and a new life.

The ship left on April 1st (with a large chunk of the hold full of Isaac's possessions). It floundered on a sandbank at Sandy Hook before getting properly underway, and Isaac Singer never saw America again.

Isaac still kept some financial interests in the new Singer Company and remained on the board of directors. This was to lead to wealth of untold proportions as Singer sewing machines swept across the world and his shares soared.

CHAPTER 42

From this point on, we leave Isaac's greatest invention in the background and follow him on the final spectacular years of his life.

On Board the SS City of Washington, in her state cabin Isabelle gave birth to their third child, Washington (named after the boat not the man) Merritt Grant Singer.

There was no need for Isaac to christen his son with the name Grant (as he had now left America), but it showed the high esteem in which he held the friendship of the General.

At 55, Isaac Singer and his entourage landed in Liverpool and then toured Europe before settling down in Paris at 83, Boulevard Malherbes.

In 1867 Isabelle gave birth to Paris Eugene Singer. Parisian society loved the family and great balls and fabulous costume dances were arranged. It was almost as if Isaac's previous colourful goings-on added to his sparkle. Of course, he was in France, where an affair or two always went down a treat with the men.

The South Bend Factory, Indiana.

Across the ocean Singer's were booming and in 1868, a brand new Singer cabinet-making factory was set up in South Bend, Indiana.

Isabelle Blanche Singer was born in Paris in 1869 and Franklin Morse Singer in February of 1870. The Singers now had six children, three French by birth, and the Singer Company was now selling over 170,000 sewing machines a year.

However, as the Singers settled into Parisian life, war was coming once more to Isaac's doorstep.

Chapter 43

Franco-Prussian War

In July of 1870 the Empire of France declared war on the Kingdom of Prussia. The problem was it did not have the forces to back up the declaration. Isaac Singer watched in horror, as the French were defeated, battle after battle. On September 2nd, Emperor Napoleon III was captured along with 100,000 of his soldiers at Sedan, which was swiftly followed by another crushing defeat at Metz, where over 180,000 French troops surrendered. The impossible was becoming a reality; Paris was in danger.

Isaac rushed to a solicitor and updated his will, as for the first time in his life he felt mortal.

Isaac decided he had seen enough war in his own country and did not want to see it again. At the last moment, Isaac managed to bribe the right officials and book passage on one of the night trains leaving the city. He quickly packed up the family, rushed to the station where pandemonium was breaking out, and with the help of guards, the family boarded one of the last safe trains out of Paris.

Troops went ahead of the train with lights to check the tracks for explosives and sabotage. Within days the capital was sure to be overrun.

By January of 1871 the family were safely in London, just as a peace treaty was signed. The Singers had left most of their clothes, furniture and possessions in Paris, thinking that they would return as soon as it was safe. However that was never to happen for Isaac.

Isaac and family tried to put down roots in London. At first this involved Brown's Hotel in Dover Street, but having six kids running around a hotel was difficult, so they moved to a grand town house just off the centre of the heaving metropolis.

Isaac kept up-to-date with news from Paris, but it was rarely good. After the peace treaty was signed an uprising followed where the Parisian's organised a revolt, which was mercilessly crushed by both French and Prussian troops. Countless thousands of Parisian's were rounded up and executed. Isaac decided he would never set foot in Paris again.

Unlike New York, the Singer family were warmly welcomed into the centre of London high society and they spent a happy summer in the capital, visiting all the attractions like Crystal Palace and the Palm House at Kew Gardens. Isaac fell in love with the home of the giant Amazonian water lily, which was warm and brilliantly engineered. He sketched the basic construction and later built a smaller version of the Kew 'glass houses' at his Palace in Paignton. Isaac loved the heat in the glass houses and hated the cold (which would eventually lead to his death).

Isaac adored the theatre and would see most of the new plays put on by Charles Dickens, or my distant grandfather, the prolific playwright, James Robinson Planché.

However, problems were brewing. The thick smog, poor sanitation and general lack of hygiene in London caused Isaac serious health problems and he became prone to chest infections. Isaac was now 60 and his boundless energy was deserting him. Also, constantly being on holiday, enjoying all the best of London had to offer, Isaac had put on considerable weight.

As summer came to an end he knew that winter in London was no place for a frail man. Isabelle was reluctant to leave, but she had also suffered health problems from the London air.

His doctors suggested that clean sea air worked for the Royal Family and would also suit Isabelle and Isaac. The warmest climate in England was the West Country, on the English Riviera, along the coast of Torquay. So once again, Isaac was quickly on the move before having to suffer freezing London a moment longer.

Chapter 44

Funnily enough, Isaac had moved around all his life, from his years as a lad on the streets to his travelling time with his own touring company. It was no problem for the big man to hit the road to find greener pastures. With his youngest child not even a year old, the family set off for the West Country.

Isaac had briefly visited the West Country before; when he disembarked from the Great Eastern in Bristol and made his way to London and later, with Isabelle on his Grand Tour.

Isaac had stayed in Exeter in 1862, so he was familiar with the area of outstanding beauty and possibly in his mind he knew where he would look first.

By February of 1872 the family took the Great Western Railway down the coast and then onto the small and bustling seaside resort of Torquay. The family moved en-mass into the new-ish and magnificent Victoria and Albert Hotel (now the Victoria in Belgrave Road). The Victoria & Albert was only a few years old and the height of Victorian elegance with a ballroom, excellent menu, orchestra and even an electric lift! Also, the top suite was self-contained with stunning coastal views and therefore perfect for Isaac and his six children.

The Victoria Hotel today still has echoes of its grand old days and is well worth a visit. If you stay there, you get a hint of its beauty from ages past, particularly when having breakfast in the main ballroom.

The Victoria & Albert Hotel in 1870.
This view is now the side entrance. Belgrave Road runs down the left to the sea.

Chapter 45

The Wigwam Begins

It was while recovering at Torquay, that Isaac made the amazing decision to shun big cities and the fast life in favour of his little hamlet on the English Riviera. Most of the locals adored him, the children loved the open sandy beaches, rocky Jurassic coastline, and freedom, and he had the fresh sea air to breathe along with plenty of sunshine.

I can just imagine the big man sitting in the sun by the sea and thinking to himself that it doesn't get any better. Torquay and the surrounding areas are still utterly beautiful. As his health improved and energy returned, Isaac was positive that it was where he wanted spend his last few years.

He sent word to London to lay off the staff at his Chelsea home and close down his town house, keeping just a skeleton staff for Isaac and Isabelle's occasional shopping trips to the big city. Isaac and Isabelle looked around for suitable land to build their magnificent palace, in which he would bring up his children and retire in wealth and happiness. He put out word to all the right people and would take Isabelle on long journeys in the hotel's pony and trap, around the small country lanes looking for suitable land. He almost found it when he came across the Brunel Estate in Torquay but fell out with the owners, exploding in his usual mad rage, before announcing he would not buy their land if there was gold on it!

On the opposite side of Torquay, across Tor-Bay on a high point 100 feet above the sea, was the Fernham-Oldway estates boasting spectacular coastal views. Even better, part of it was for sale! Bingo. When Isaac visited he immediately loved the site, gesturing to Isabelle where everything would be built and how it would lay with every main window showing panoramic views to the sea.

Land and property was soon rented (and then purchased), and Isaac moved a stone's throw along the coast to the sleepy hamlet of Paignton. He and the family moved into two properties on the elevated land of the Oldway Estate, which backed onto open farmland. The land was perfect and there was more available to buy all around the estate.

However, the houses, or rather villas at Little Oldway were small in comparison to what he wanted, (one is now a retirement home). Isaac immediately set about enlarging them to suit his temporary needs while he planned his palace.

Isaac was soon overseeing the clearance of the old apple orchards, gardens and remaining properties. Six cottages were flattened, and a pub, barns and some other warehousing were demolished, leaving a huge barren plateau above the sea.

Plans were being drawn up along the lines of some of the amazing architecture that he had seen on his tours of Europe. Remember Isaac was rich beyond any imaginings and getting richer by the hour, as his sewing machines went global. His brilliant deal with Clark back at Singer headquarters meant that Isaac got a cut of everything. Money was simply no object.

Isaac's dream was to build a palace on a grand scale. He wanted to call it his 'Wigwam' as a little joke to his American roots, however the property ended up with several titles; Oldway House, Oldway Manor, Oldway Palace, Oldway Hall or simply, Oldway. Around the area it was always referred to as Mr Singer's Palace. Whatever it was called, Isaac, and later his son, Paris, made sure that Oldway was to become a real palace on par with many around Europe, including Blenheim and Buckingham Palace. Even the faded glory of what is left standing today takes your breath away.

Isaac called on the expertise of a 31year old architect, George Soudon Bridgman, who had just finished designing the impressive Torbay Hotel in Torquay.

Isaac had a dream of building a house on his cleared plateau that was so unique it would be compared with the best in the world. Isabelle had some input as well, and between them, and later their children, a dream would come true.

Isaac and Isabelle knew what they wanted; he was a designer and inventor. He had also built his own properties before and seen just about every grand house in Europe, including King George's palace at Brighton, now called Brighton Pavilion.

Chapter 46

As one of the richest men in the world, Isaac would design and build his 'Wigwam', which by any standards would be a palace of extraordinary quality and proportions. Although Isaac personally called his home 'Wigwam' the name Oldway persisted, so in the end Isaac changed the name of his home in his will from Wigwam to Oldway.

Stone was shipped in from Portland, and granite from Aberdeen, hundreds of windows would be framed with terracotta coloured bricks and the great Singer 'S' monogram (that was on every sewing machine Singer's made), would grace the front of the building like a heraldic shield. The property would have touches of all the great houses of Europe. First to go up was the Rotunda started in 1871, but as soon as that was sorted all the plans and materials for the main building were finalised, The Wigwam started to rise like a colossus above Paignton.

On the 10 May 1873 a grand event was laid on. As all the workmen surrounded the Singer family, Isabelle laid the first foundation stone of their palace. With great cheering, hundreds of workmen started to build one of the most impressive properties in the West of England.

The front driveway would actually sweep up to the first floor, entering through four grand Palladian pillars into the Italianate hall. In the hall, just by the entrance to his special theatre, would be Singer's first Jenny Lind sewing machine with his patent drawings in a huge display cabinet.

Isaac sent Bridgman off to Paris to get structural details of some of the properties and palaces that he adored, and then set about adding every latest invention that could be put into his new dream home. Isaac drew from all his experiences for, what was in reality, his mausoleum. He loved Claridges in London, where great heads of state regularly stayed. He loved parts of Hampton Court and many other great buildings, scribbling endless ideas down for his architects and designers.

Isaac also commissioned a huge totem pole to stand at the front of the building with a Red Indian firing an arrow from a bow,

This is a drawing of just a part of Isaac's Wigwam, published in the periodicals of the day. A huge S was emblazoned in the stonework like some heraldic shield. Isaac Singer would not live to see his precious Wigwam completed.

to further support his preferred home name, 'Wigwam'. Many years later, his son Paris donated the Indian pole to Paignton, where it stood above the bandstand on the seafront.

Isaac would also incorporate a large theatre designed by Frank Matcham, who was probably related to the main building contractor, James Matcham, from Plymouth. Frank went on to become one of the greatest theatre designers of his time.

The theatre is where Isaac and his children would put on plays to entertain visitors and the people of Paignton and Torquay.

Isaac's hate of the cold would be conquered by central heating. A few years before, one of his friends and fellow sewing machines pioneers, Allen Benjamin Wilson, partner in the famous Wheeler & Wilson company and fellow member of the infamous Sewing Machine Cartel, had designed his own boilers and heating for his home in Waterbury, Connecticut.

Wilson had completed his house and then went on to build a hotel called Wilson House in North Adams, Massachusetts, which also contained a theatre, but more importantly it was fully central heated.

In 1865, the year before Isaac had left America, Isaac was given the grand tour of the almost completed hotel, where Wilson proudly displayed his new-fangled boiler and radiators. It was this idea that Isaac used to keep his Wigwam warm, whatever the weather.

Chapter 47

The next four years of Singer's life were his happiest. It is here that we see the dramatic change in character from the fighter who had struggled to feed himself, to the father and benevolent old man for which he is still fondly remembered in Paignton.

He was known to donate to the local churches and charities and help the destitute with food, shelter and work.

Isaac regularly held great feasts for the less affluent so that they could eat as much as they liked. All the family would join in and it was a great grounding for Isaac's children who had so much, to mix with the normal men and women who had to struggle for their daily bread.

While over 200 workmen and professionals were building the main manor at an impressive rate, Isaac also designed and had started The Arena, or Rotunda, next to the grand house.

The Rotunda looked like a huge circular stone Bedouin tent. All the time Isaac, who was still in his villa on site, overlooked everything like some ancient pharaoh building his tomb. His fantastic memory for names came in handy as he toured his

Oldway Manor, Paignton, taken by me in 2012.
This is the side of Oldway where Isaac Singer died shortly after one of his children's weddings. Apparently it had around 110 rooms, with a hall of mirrors modelled on many of the great homes like Coleridge's in London or parts of Hampton Court and Versailles, especially the gardens. Oldway Manor is presently owned by the local council, who upkeep and cherish the unique property that they have inherited. The decoration inside takes your breath away.

buildings daily, chatting to the workmen, joking and laughing with them.

The Rotunda was mainly used for horse training, which Isaac followed with a passion, and his son, Franklin, carried on breeding some of the finest bloodstock in Europe. However, in the evening the Rotunda could be converted into a fantastic showpiece for entertainment.

The doors were large enough to allow a coach and horses straight in, to unload out of the rain so as not to spoil the ladies'

The Rotunda equestrian centre and entertainment venue still survives today, but is in desperate need of restoration.

evening gowns. The Rotunda survives to this day but is only a shadow of its former glory, when great parties were laid on and Isaac and his children performed for the local population before his theatre was completed.

The Wigwam and the Rotunda both survive in Paignton, part Council Offices, part empty, but well worth a visit if you are ever in the vicinity. It is not hard to imagine the grandeur of the palace in its heyday, with Isaac's children running around and staff everywhere.

The Rotunda was completed in record time as Isaac paid his workmen top wages and treated them well. He only had one condition, which was non-negotiable; he had used it in his sewing machine factories to great effect. If a strike were to be called, for any reason, Isaac would shut up shop, lay everyone off, leave, and never return.

Fair enough, most of the locals thought. With Isaac Singer's investment in the town, Paignton was growing at a rapid rate and everyone was benefitting from the baker to the candlestick-maker. Paignton was being nicknamed Singerton.

While he may have been shunned by America, the wealth that he brought to the West Country of England was most welcome. Singer employed hundreds of local workmen on his palace and he became a popular sight around the town. He was like a mafia don, an all-powerful, strange and imposing giant of a man in the sleepy backwater of old England. People would stop work and bow or tap their hats as he passed, and occasionally, he would stop and chat before continuing.

Isaac had special carriages commissioned for his home, travelling, and the races and would often be seen flying around in them. He had clothes sent from London that only he could get away with; bright silks and satins, velvets and cashmere suits. On a local they would have looked ridiculous, but they suited the big American to a T.

Unfortunately, even with his great eye for racing bloodstock and seemingly limitless wealth, Isaac never fitted in with the local upper classes. They shunned many of his great events, but Isaac was surrounded by a thong of eager and happy locals only too willing to fill his house with laughter and gaiety at every opportunity.

Chapter 48

Birthday Celebrations at Oldway

It was during 1873 that Isaac sent for one of his favourite children from a previous relationship. He had pestered Alice Eastwood Merritt Walter, daughter of Isaac and Mary Eastwood Walter (known for a while as Mrs Merritt), for some time and eventually she agreed to come to England.

Alice had many of Isaac's traits – she was by all accounts a beautiful woman and had a penchant for acting. After a huge journey across the world, the young girl duly arrived at the manor. It was a day of great joy for Isaac, who openly wept in front of his workmen, then fell to his knees as he met her coming up the path.

She soon joined in with the other children and became part of his Paignton family. In fact she fitted in so well that Isaac and Isabelle's daughter, Winnaretta, later acted as one of her bridesmaids when she married in July of 1875.

On October 27 1873 Isaac and family put on a showpiece to celebrate his 62nd birthday. Enough of the house and stage was completed to hold an evening of fantastic entertainment, complete with an accompanying pianoforte.

Alice Merritt, now with the surname Singer, played the maid of the Rising Sun Tavern, from Offenbach's comic opera, in a one-act piece called *Breaking the Spell*.

Winnie performed a solo scene, Spooning the Sands. Mortimer Singer, now dropping the Adam from his name altogether, did a scene between Cardinal Wolsey and Cromwell from *Henry VIII* and then, not to be outdone, did a solo piece, Courting in the Rain.

The evening was a great success and unlike New York the place was packed to the rafters. Everyone in the vicinity, (excluding a few snobs), attended.

And so Isaac Singer settled into his retirement with ease, enjoying his family and wealth.

On January 1st 1874 the Rotunda was complete and ready for its first great event. A huge New Year celebration was held.

In the New Year, children from the surrounding villages and the workmen's kids were invited into the newly completed Rotunda. As they walked inside the amazing building, the likes of which they had never seen before, a band welcomed them in.

In the centre was the most enormous Christmas tree they had ever seen, reaching high into the building. It was decked from top-to-toe with presents, hundreds of them, some even say over

Isaac Merritt Singer in his final year, dressed in silk and crimson velvet, still a grand and imposing man with white flowing hair, but as he told his friends his appearance was deceptive; he felt hollow and constantly fatigued. He was now famous for his children's parties and charitable donations. He had come a long way since he wore ripped jackets, holed shoes and stole food to survive.
(Photograph with kind permission from the PDC, Paignton).

a thousand were piled at its base. As the children played games they were allowed to open their presents, and for some it was the greatest day of their lives.

As the evening continued, dancing and feasting in the main house followed for the parents and other guests.

One final incident at Oldway that I was told about, shook family life. I was not sure about this at first, but then bells started to ring after I found out a bit about Isaac's will, so it may well have grounding in reality rather than rumour.

Allegedly, Isaac was in ill health and was slowly walking through part of his mansion with new instruction for some door openings, when he entered a room still under construction. In the room he found Isabelle and one of the performing artists who was there for a show. Isaac, (the ultimate womaniser who knew every trick), immediately recognised the compromising situation that Isabelle and the artist were in and flew into a rage. He sacked the man on the spot and brought all work to a standstill at his new home.

Some say it was Alice's future husband, the handsome Monsieur La Grove and interestingly their marriage only lasted a matter of days, for as soon as Isaac had died, all hell exploded at the house and La Grove hit the road for America. We can only guess as to what happened and what caused the permanent rift between the two newlyweds.

Apparently Isabelle wriggled out of the serious situation and managed to subdue the old man. More images of King Henry

VIII and Catherine Parr spring to mind.

As work resumed on his palace Isaac summoned his local solicitor and good family friend, Yard Eastley, who contacted his New York friend and lawyer, David Hawley.

Rumour had it that Isaac was going to add a codicil to his will, stating that if after his death, Isabelle were ever to marry again, she would immediately lose any title to Oldway and its lands. This would be a crushing blow to Isabelle as she had put so much of her heart into the buildings.

Because of his constant visits, Isaac became good friends with a local doctor, who not only looked after him, but also became executor for his will. Isaac made sure that Dr Charles William Pridham would, along with Eastley and Hawley in New York, have control of his trusts and estates after his death.

Chapter 49

Alice's Wedding

Isaac was now in failing health and even with the sea air and the best London doctor, Sir William Jenner, his days were numbered. Isaac set his mind on trying to reach his 65th birthday in October of 1875, but even with expert help, it soon became clear that he was not going to make it.

Pridham would have told the straight-talking Isaac, during his regular visits, that his time was near. During Isaac's final summer he set about designing a memorial to suit his personality, a large and impressive tomb. Isaac also took the time to design an amazing coffin fit for a king.

Isaac Singer's coffin was impressive. Actually there were three coffins fitting one-inside-the-other, like a Russian doll. The coffin in which he was to lay was going to be made of lime but he changed his mind and ordered cedar. He had it lined in pure white satin and silk with hand-woven Maltese Lace in ruffled layers. The second outer-coffin was made of really thick lead, twice the normal thickness. The final outside show-coffin was impressive and had to be huge to accommodate the other two.

Don't forget Isaac, was a large figure of a man at six foot five and overweight, some say well over 20 stone. The last coffin was made of solid English Oak and decorated with pure silver filigree work and large solid silver extra strong handles. Once finished to Isaac's approval, a marble tomb was designed to take its huge size.

There are very few photographs of the great man himself as photography was still a relatively new idea in 1875. However this is one of the rare pictures of Isaac and his presidents. He is in his huge conservatory, which stretched around the palace that he called his Wigwam. Isaac can be seen here signing some papers for the Singer Company with a dip-pen. Within a few months of this photo the legend was dead. McKenzie is in the middle and the much younger Hopper is on the right. Hopper died very young, aged 45 in 1881, though he had resigned from Singer's the year after Isaac's death.
Don't you love the huge mutton chops!

Isaac was too weak on 14 July 1875 to walk his favourite daughter, Alice down the aisle. He had already postponed the wedding while an infection he had rumbled on, but as he realised he was not going to get better the date was set.

Isaac's American lawyer, David Hawley, had travelled across the world to help with finalising his complicated and enormous estate, and he was even working on Isaac's will the morning of the wedding.

Isaac was in a very poor state when he put his wobbly mark on his final codicil.

David had kindly agreed to take Alice's arm and walk her down the aisle. Isaac had caught a summer cold and had been suffering with a severe chest inflammation that had weakened his already failing heart even more, so he needed constant rest. Although he could not walk with Alice, he was apparently propped up in a huge chair for the occasion, but was lifted to his bed shortly after and missed the reception.

Alice was marrying a handsome French-American called William Alonso Paul La Grove, from New York. Alice was wearing Isaac's wedding present to her, a stunning set of diamonds costing £2,347, hand made for her by the Royal Jewellers, Asprey's in London. Today they would be worth the price of a house. I wonder who has them now? The earrings were just one of the many presents that Isaac showered his best loved daughter with, and it makes you wonder if La Grove was only after an enormous pay off.

By all accounts their wedding was simply spectacular; except for a royal wedding, nothing came close and no expense was spared. I wonder if that caused a rift with Isaac's other children at the time? Certainly the next few weeks saw an enormous eruption at the family home.

Alice was dressed in a long white satin dress that was trimmed with handmade Brussels lace, dotted with orange flowers. They say her dress cost the same as a London apartment! Her carriage was sumptuously decorated for the trip to the church. Six bridesmaids, including Winnaretta, followed Alice down the aisle at St John's Church, and later an amazing wedding feast was held at Oldway.

I wonder if Isaac could hear all the frivolities echoing around his huge mansion, as he lay alone, breathing heavily, in his presidential bed.

Chapter 50

Death of a Pioneer

Nine days after Alice's wedding, as evening closed in on 23rd July 1875, Isaac Singer lay in his great bed, surrounded by his family and doctors. Isaac received communion as his breathing slowed and as the last light of day faded, his heart finally gave out. All the hardships of his early struggles had taken their toll, as had his over-indulgences in later life. Dr Pridham confirmed his death just before 10pm. Isaac was 64.

The greatest sewing machine pioneer in the history of the world had died. The next morning Yard Eastley rode to Exeter to record Isaac's death.

Isaac's funeral was spectacular – even more so when all the workmen who had feared for their jobs, were informed that Isaac had left strict instructions in his will (and plenty of money), to see his dream house completed.

He was deeply mourned and his funeral was almost like a state funeral, with nearly 80 black carriages pulled by countless horses, some specially shipped in from France. It was certainly the most expensive and spectacular funeral in the history of the West Country.

Isaac's body was dressed immaculately; his white hair and combed beard lay over his pristine Indian cotton shirt with favourite signature gold cufflinks. He had on a tie pin and his gold Albert chain draped across his tailor made satin waistcoat and finally his black trousers and long black coat. He was placed in his spectacular hand-built coffin and taken up to the house by the undertakers to be laid in state in the ballroom at Oldway.

Rumours later grew of the amount of gold that Isaac had around his body, and many years later, in 1974, thieves broke into Isaac's tomb. Although they were arrested and punished no one ever revealed what they found.

On the day of the funeral a large cortège set out from the mansion led by one of the undertakers, Prebendary Hall with Dr McKenzie in the first carriage. Isaac's hearse followed behind, pulled by two bay horses. Behind them followed his children and more carriages with some of his workmen and estate manager. Behind them followed many men on foot and more carriages. For reasons that I have yet to discover, Winnaretta did not attend the funeral. It is possible that she was heartbroken as her diary entries of the time are tear-filled pages for the loss of her 'dear Papa'.

At Torquay Railway Station there were many more people and carriages waiting. Most of the businesses had closed for the day out of respect and all flags were flown at half-mast. You have to remember that Isaac had almost single-handedly brought amazing prosperity to the area.

Thousands of mourners and onlookers jammed the streets as the procession slowly marched to his final resting place, at the top of the hill in Torquay. Papers noted that the procession was so long it stretched all the way from the seafront to the cemetery in an unbroken line. While Isaac was laid in his final resting place there were still some carriages in line down on the seafront. There were over 2,000 mourners just in the cortège. It seemed as if the whole of the West Country had turned up, for Isaac's funeral was not to be missed.

Isaac Merritt Singer is buried in Torquay Cemetery, opposite Torquay Crematorium at the top of the town. The entrance is in Barton Road. If you would like to find his tomb, walk up from the entrance toward the boarded-up chapel near the top. You will see his huge white tomb on the right. It is crammed with information and many of his relatives are with him.

There is no church at the cemetery where Isaac rests in eternal peace; only a small dilapidated chapel, and I often wonder if this is because of his reputation. Before his death he had given generously to the parish church and had a priest at his deathbed. I am sure he would have wanted to have a church burial, but who would allow such a man in their cemetery in 1875. The morals and standards of the day were very different to today. History states that Isaac's mausoleum was just too large to be in any of the local church cemeteries. Can that really be true?

As I write, the cemetery is in appalling condition, with many graves being vandalised, smashed or toppled. Strangely Isaac's impressive white marble tomb is untouched, as is his son's behind him.

Isaac Singer's final resting place in Torquay is a white marble tomb. It is so large that it makes me look small, which is no mean feat! The angel behind is also part of the Singer/Vanderbilt family.

And so, the most famous of all entrepreneurs was dead. Isaac Singer had blazed a trail that would never be followed, and had lived life to the full.

Let me remind you why I say 'never to be followed'. While

Isaac Singer's early life was spent in poverty and obscurity, his final years were spent in a blaze of wealth and publicity.

Isaac Singer invented the first useful sewing machine in the history of the world. He helped pioneer proper mass production, pioneered hire purchase, oversaw the first patent pooling and had one of the first truly multi-national companies, employing nearly 100,000 people. Singer machines were the first mass-marketed domestic appliances in the world, and may just go down in history as the most useful invention of the 19th century.

Singer's were the first company to spend over one million dollars on advertising in one year. This, along with superb machines like the New Family machine of 1865, made Singer machines world leaders. They dominated the world market selling 80% of all sewing machines made in 1900.

And, moreover, when Isaac died as a grey haired old man, he was married to the most beautiful woman in Europe.

He really did start from nothing, with little more than the clothes on his back. Singer was what the American Dream was all about. The son of an immigrant, he made the first good sewing machine in history, whatever other makers may tell you. But the ultimate capitalist's story does not end here.

Isaac was the patriarch of a massive and rapidly expanding family, a family that went on to fill newspapers the world over with exploits from horse breeding to public affairs.

Chapter 51

The King is Dead, Long Live the King
Isaac's Will

When I first managed to set eyes on Isaac's will, it was a 'eureka' moment. I felt like I should have been wearing white cotton gloves as I gazed in awe at his last words, written shortly before his death. His hand-written will, in three parts, referred back to his earlier version, which he set out in July of 1870 while escaping from Paris, and also to his codicil, set out in August 1873, where he was still referring to his home as The Wigwam, not Oldway. Rather than revoke his earlier two wills Isaac simply added a codicil to bring it all up to date.

Firstly, and clearly at the forefront on his mind was his expensive funeral, in which all costs were to be covered and paid. The showman was to go out in style. Secondly, his beloved Oldway; Isaac left instructions for the completion of his palace, including funds for its decoration and furnishing, all to be overseen by Isabelle.

Isaac left an enormous amount in his will worth countless

millions in today's money, mainly in stocks, bonds, property and of course, his shares in the ever expanding Singer Company. When his estate was published the world was dumbstruck that this self-made man could have possibly generated such a sum in a single lifetime.

Even after all his frivolous spending, his estate was estimated at well over £8,000,000 and was growing by the day! When the average wage was a few shillings a week Isaac's fortune was breath-taking.

In his will, Isaac Singer left his houses, property and all their contents, even the carriages and garden statues, in trust to Isabelle, to be split equally amongst the surviving children once they reached 21. Isabelle could stay in the house for the rest of her life (with a little codicil on that, which we shall see shortly). Isaac even took the precaution to allow a part of his estate to any unborn child of his, born to Isabelle after his death. Had Isabelle told him she was pregnant again? Oh, how I would have loved to be a fly on the wall in the final days of the old sewing machine king.

He then generously split his enormous wealth among his many surviving children, naming over 20 of them individually and making most of them rich.

Rumours also persist that he left money to some of his wives and even mistresses via separate undisclosed agreements, and even secretly to two Paignton women! I have never tracked any of these documents down but several of Isaac's early women certainly seem to have flourished after his death.

Interestingly, many years after Isaac's death, Paris Singer employed a tall and handsome local lad, who had many of Isaac's characteristics. Gossip was that the lad was an offspring of Isaac's last conquest in the town, which seems unlikely, but you can never tell with old Isaac.

Over the following months there were several claims for a slice of his fortune by other children, which largely ended up in protracted court cases. Had DNA testing been around we may have found out just to what extent Isaac Singer was a ladies' man! For example, much to Isabelle's astonishment, he had still been quietly paying support to Mary McGonigal and Mary Walter back in America.

Isabelle knew that any delay would stop the money being released from Isaac's will, so she acted quickly to sort out problems so that it could proceed as smoothly as possible. She managed to convince all the people receiving money from Isaac, to pool their resources for a fighting fund, to sort out whoever was holding things up.

Catherine Haley, Isaac's first wife saw an opportunity, and stuck her oar into the proceedings. Both William and Lillian C Singer (his first two children with Catherine), had been left smaller amounts by Isaac. This was because he could never really forgive them for deserting him and taking Catherine's side when he was in trouble. However Isabelle made sure they received $90,000 between them from the estate. That enormous sum seemed to work like a charm.

Catherine was not even mentioned in Isaac's will, so the estate quickly paid out $60,000 to make her go away. The huge amount paid showed that she might have had some real evidence to delay probate.

Catherine eventually retired to Brooklyn, New York, dying in 1884. She is buried in Greenwood Cemetery.

One massive fly in the ointment was Isaac's old mistress, Mary Ann Sponsler, who had again came back to haunt him. On hearing of his death, she immediately filed a claim, stating that she was Isaac's legitimate wife at the time that Isabelle had married Isaac, and therefore due his estate. This was nonsense as she had already gone through a sham divorce.

Now her case was sneakily simple; because her divorce from Isaac had not been settled legally, her marriage to John Foster must therefore be illegal, and therefore, Isaac's marriage to Isabelle must also be illegal.

In Mary Ann's mind she was the only legitimate wife of Isaac Singer, and so was accordingly entitled to a portion of his wealth. It sounds quite feasible, the only problem being that she had never married Isaac in the first place.

Against just about all the advice from friends and family, Mary Ann ploughed ahead and opened a can of worms that has never closed.

If she could win her case, true or not, this could make her rich. Isabelle had tried to cut Mary Ann off at the pass, as had Clark, (who quickly reinserted himself back at Singer's, now the big man had gone). They offered Mary Ann huge amounts, rising in increments to over a quarter of a million dollars as the court case drew nearer, but she was after the pot of gold and she told her lawyers to settle for no less than $4,000,000.

The papers loved it. In court Mary Ann could finally destroy Isaac, if not the man himself, then his memory forever. She divulged every bit of dirt she could come up with and the papers printed it all, with the usual enhancements of course.

This slaughter of Isaac's character worked perfectly and he has been unfairly cast as the evil villain in the Singer saga ever since. I can hear a groan coming from Isaac's grave as I write!

After weeks in court, the periodicals portrayed the powerful Singer family and the Singer Company on one side, and the poor betrayed Mary Ann on the other. She was magnificent in her ignominy, playing the downtrodden and shamed wife. Oh, the embarrassment of it all! But even with all of her acting, the judge pointed out that one crucial point; she never married Isaac, and she was legally married to another man. The judge was not swayed, unlike the previous judge who had awarded her a ridiculously large alimony without a real case. He pointed out that he could not change the law to suit her feelings, the case was dismissed without a penny and she endured huge legal costs.

Mary Ann left court furious, and immediately appealed the ruling of the Surrogate's Court in the Supreme Court. She lost again, and although she had gambled everything, she must have taken some bitter comfort in knowing that she had destroyed

Isaac's character for all time.

From that day on, every reference book, history book, every paper and writer who ever wrote a word about Isaac Singer, would write it in the shadow of Mary Ann's bitter and biased portrayal.

Mary Ann may not have won any money, but she did have many children who were left huge sums in Isaac's will, so she did live comfortably for the rest of her life. Mary Ann died in 1896.

CHAPTER 52

Back at the Singer Company, Edward Clark took the opportunity to work on Inslee Hooper, who was in failing health and would later die from sheer exhaustion worn out at the young age of 45.

Clark, still a majority shareholder, removed Hooper and became president of Singer's in 1876. Isaac's old sparring partner had finally fulfilled his lifelong dream. I bet on the day he managed that, he stood in the huge Singer President's office and smiled to himself.

Edward Clark had a rewarding and successful career, and in 1880 it culminated in the design and production of his impressive Dakota building in the upper west side of Manhattan. Both Isaac and Edward had been investing in land around the area before Isaac's departure for Europe.

Back in 1880, there were no other buildings around as it grew from the foundations. Clark's home was just far enough from town to avoid the smells and heat of a bustling city and the perfect place to spend his final years.

Unfortunately for Clark, he died in October of 1882 aged 71, after contracting typhoid from drinking infected water, two years before the buildings completion. The massive drain on his wealth may have contributed to his demise. However he still died with a vast fortune, some say over 25 million dollars, which he left to his only son, Alfred. Caroline, his wife had died several years earlier.

As a final twist, legend says that Edward Clark still haunts the basement of the Dakota Buildings and has been seen there several times, I wonder why the basement? Perhaps that is where he was infected!

Edward Clark's Dakota building is far better known today as the site where John Lennon lived and was assassinated.

Chapter 53

Isaac had basically added up his total fortune and then split it into equal parts, which he distributed as he desired. Nearly all of his offspring received a cut, except Violetta, whose husband, William Fash Proctor as Isaac carefully explained in his will, had already acquired a small fortune from the Singer Company. I bet that must have caused a few words!

William, Isaac's oldest son, who had gone through so much with his father got a real slap in the face with a single payment of $500 (before Isabelle stepped in). This was a serious piece of psychology from Isaac. Had Isaac left William out of his will completely, William could easily console himself that his idiot father had so many children, it was just an oversight, an error, a simple mistake from an ailing old man. Isaac was anything but a fool, there was a legal loophole that he was trying to avoid. If William had been left out of his will entirely, it would have opened up the will to be challenged in court. However, by leaving William a pitiful sum, Isaac was sending his son a message from the grave. When Isaac had come to William many years earlier and asked him for help with his divorce (against William's mother Catherine), William refused. It had broken something inside Isaac; his eldest beloved son had turned his back on him when he needed him most, and Isaac had never forgiven him. Leaving William a pittance showed there was no mistake; he had not forgotten him or what his first born had done.

William's sister, Lillian, was also left a one off payment of $10,000, but Isabelle soon realised that this would cause a huge wedge in the Singer family and probably delay probate further, so she soon sorted both William and Lillian out to help things along.

To Isabelle and his six legitimate children in England, Isaac bequeathed the lion's share. Isabelle received four parts of the estate, the boys received six parts each, and the girl's five parts each. Once his children came of age they would be independently rich beyond their wildest dreams.

As soon as the will was sworn true in September of 1875, David Hawley travelled to Liverpool and booked passage aboard a sailing ship bound for New York, where he would start the ball rolling in America with Isaac's other children. Little did he know there would be a storm waiting for him and several drawn out court cases.

Because of all the delays in Isaac's will, it took three hard years to get it passed probate. His will was finally (now double probate), re-sworn true and passed in March 1878 in Exeter, England. This allowed the executors to control the outflow of money, lands, property and shares to each individual named in Isaac's complex will. Over 21 of his children received their portion of his inheritance in the form of trusts and financial payouts.

One family member told me that a large chunk of European royalty today is running wild with the blood of Isaac Singer's Jewish Catholics.

Chapter 54

Isabelle Eugenie Boyer
Part 3
Vicomtesse d'e Estenburgh

I just have to add a chapter of what Singer's last wife got up to. It is brilliant.

Isabelle, now worth millions, carried on with the completion of the house, and for a while, a few of Isaac's generous ways, but she soon got bored.

When the house was finished, cartloads of seaweed was moved up from the shore to fertilise the impressive new gardens, which were full of fountains and statues like some Roman villa.

The Oldway Estate steward, Mr McCormack, oversaw it all. Although William McCormack was quite young when he started at Oldway, he managed both the Paignton estate and their property in Chelsea, London.

William McCormack went on to have 12 children, with seven

of them being born at Oldway.

To celebrate the completion of Oldway, Isabelle held a grand opening party. Isabelle was still a young and attractive woman and life for her as a widow would become dull in the West Country, now that the great man was no longer there to attract the famous and important people.

As I mentioned earlier, there had been a little codicil on Isaac's will which clearly stated that she may live at the house, as long as she was unmarried and she kept it in good order.

The trustees had been handing out money for its upkeep as needed, but it must have been a struggle for her as her correspondence with them used polite but threatening semantics.

By 1878, Isabelle had decided enough was enough. She had big plans and she was going to put them into action. She yearned for the exciting hustle and bustle of her old Parisian life and made the decision that life, as a widow in a palace by herself, would not work. She told the family to pack for Paris.

This caused huge rows, as many of the children regarded Oldway as their home. Isabelle tried to explain to the children, that to marry well they needed to be in society, not locked away in rural England where there was a glut of farmers! This did little to persuade them.

After much bitter wrangling a date was set for the family to leave, before winter set in.

However, Mortimer Singer had other plans. Mortimer was a young man now, and although he gave up trying to argue with his mother when the time came, he could not face leaving his home.

The story goes that as Isabelle and all the children boarded the coach bound for Paignton Station, Mortimer disappeared into the darkness and could not be found. The decision was made to leave without him and get him sent on once he was caught up with.

Mortimer had walked in the dark, down to where Isaac's old friend, Eastley lived, banged on his door and begged him to let him stay the night.

Yard Eastley allowed Mortimer to stay and also pointed out to him that, according to Isaac's will, he was now financially secure for life. Basically Mortimer could do what he liked.

Now, gossip goes that Isabelle, who had put on many social evenings at Oldway, had fallen for one of the musicians that came to perform at the grand house. He, like many musicians was talented, specialising in singing and playing the violin, but he was earning a meagre living from touring and performing.

Victor Reubsaet may have been the reason Isabelle was so desperate to get to Paris. On 8 January 1879, not long after her arrival, she married Victor. And allegedly, not long after that, her new husband saw her children's inheritance as a honey pot to be sampled!

As per Isaac's will, Isabelle once remarried, would never again be allowed to live in Oldway, though she did visit several times to see the children who had returned home.

Rumour goes that her new husband had turned to the children, to try and wiggle their fortunes away from them before they turned 21 and had full control. This caused a huge rift in the family and was one of the reasons why some of the children returned to England; securing with the help of Yard Eastley, their fortunes against any future attacks.

Isabelle's time in Paris was a blur of entertaining, marriage, investments and buying a few titles for her new husband to ensure that he would be accepted in society. Nothing makes people turn their heads quicker than beautiful people with impressive titles.

It was while Isabelle was living the high life, after years of being stifled, legend says she modelled naked for Bartholdi's Statue of Liberty, and although some said she did not, she boasted openly about it for many years, often striking the pose at dinner parties.

Although Isabelle married Victor Reubsaet, who was completely penniless, she soon set about changing his image with a few titles.

It is possible that Victor's real name was **Jan Nicolas Reubsaet**. Son of Jean Baptist Victor Reubsaet, he was born in the Dutch town of Sittard on 26 April 1843. Victor was the son of a shoemaker, and with Isabelle's money they bought the title of **Vicomte de 'Estembourg (Estenburgh) de Bloemdaal** from the Austrian Emperor.

Well is one title enough? From the Italian King Umberto, in 1881, they also purchased the grand title of **Duce de Camposelice or Compostella**.

The rich couple bought titles and property and set Europe alight with glamorous entertaining. Victor died in September of 1887. Isabelle married once again to one Paul Sohege and died in Paris in 1904 at the age of 62.

Chapter 55

Oldway

Oldway went through the years in an astounding number of costumes. Initially the three boys, Mortimer, Paris and Washington, moved back to Paignton and they all lived as neighbours, living in fine houses of which some are still hotels in the area.

They partied at Oldway and spent much of their trust funds on the latest must-have's, like fine horses and carriages, parties, and later cars.

Washington and Paris managed to buy Oldway outright from the other trustees around 1893, and a few years later Paris moved back into his father's estate. Paris then bought out Washington and owned Oldway outright. He had big plans for the palace.

In 1904, after the death of his mother, Paris Singer implemented a massive facelift of Oldway to make it more to his own tastes. He added huge Palladian pillars all along the front and changed the gardens. Apparently Paris Singer loved the Palace at

Versailles and copied not only the interior, such as the ballroom and grand stairs, but he also organised castings to be made from the garden statues so they could be replicated. Oldway became known as the 'Mini Versailles of the West'.

Paris Singer, like his father, loved cutting edge technology, and after successfully installing electricity into Oldway, he then helped do the same in Sandringham, bringing the stately home of the Royal Family into the modern age.

By 1910, the Oldway that stands today was complete.

When the First World War raged the house was used as the American Women's War Hospital, which is not as the title implies, for American women, but used by American women to look after wounded servicemen throughout the war.

Paris Singer was at the train station, along with his daughter, also named Winnaretta, to help with the first wounded.

Amongst the young nurses in Torquay was one who would help out with the operations and in the pharmacy. She later went on to be the best-selling crime novelist of all time, Agatha Christie.

Queen Mary even came to inspect Oldway, which had all the latest equipment including an X-ray machine.

In 1939, Oldway was taken over by the Royal Air Force on orders from the Home Office. Oldway became No 4 Wing of the RAF for officer training. Not a bad place to learn, eh! Even King George VI popped in to check it out.

In 1946, in accordance Paris Singer's earlier wishes, the Singer family sold Oldway to Paignton Council, at a price of £46,000.

Throughout the decades the house underwent many changes, at one point becoming a country club, and then a civic centre, where you could even have your own wedding.

Since 1948, Torbay Council has used Oldway as offices. There are rumours afoot that the mansion is to be turned into a hotel. If they do I'll be booking the first room!

What is left of the gardens is well maintained, and a bowling club and tennis club have the use of part of it. Unfortunately, the trees have grown up around the fringe of the land, and these large weeds have stolen the amazing views that Isaac first fell in love with. His workmen spent nearly a year just clearing the plateau to make sure Isaac had the best vista possible. The growth also hides Oldway from visitors, who often have trouble finding the landmark.

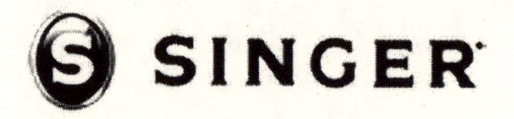

SINGER

Chapter 56

Isaac Singer's Women and Known Children

Researching Isaac's kids has been a bit of a nightmare as he made up names and assumed different identities to hide his illicit behaviour. What I always say with absolute certainty is, that no one knows exactly how many mistresses Isaac Singer had or indeed, how many children.

What I have done is start a list of known children for your interests or research. Hey, it only took me 30 years to get this far. I bet you could do it on the Internet in a month now! Oh how I cry...

Several of Singer's wealthy children went on to marry into high society, some into European high-class families. Some took up important positions around the world. A few even carried on in their father's wandering ways...

Let's have a summary of his known wives, mistresses and kids that we know about.

1st wife, Catherine Maria Haley
Children
William Singer 1834-1914
Lillian Singer 1837
Catherine was married to Isaac Singer between 1830 and 1860 though the last few years they spent apart.

Mary Ann Sponsler
Children
Isaac Augustus (called Junior by his dad but Gus by the rest of the family)
Violetta Teresa (became Mrs Proctor)
John Albert
Fanny Elizabeth (married William Archer)
Jasper Hamlet
Mary Olive (married Sturges Whitlock)
Julia Ann,
Caroline Virginia
Two others, sadly died young.

Mary McGonigal, (worked at Singer's) **known as Mrs Matthews and for a time Mrs Merritt-Matthews**
Children
Ruth Merritt (1852)
Clara, Florence Adelaide
Margaret Alexandra
Charles Alexander (1859) named after Isaac's son who had died
Two more sadly died (one in 1854). All Isaac's children with Mary received two portions of his will, worth a fortune.

Mary Lived at 70 Christopher Street, New York under the name Matthews with her children and her sister Kate, but she possibly moved back to San Francisco after Isaac left America.

I believe Isaac and Mary McGonigal's daughter Ruth, who went under the name of Ruth Merritt Matthews, may have died in childbirth around the same time as her father, in 1875. Although she was left a large sum in Isaac's will, her inheritance went to Charles Hopkins, her husband. Charles Hopkins already owned a substantial stake in the Singer Company. When Charles H Hopkins died in 1913 he was so wealthy that his inheritance tax set a new record for the state of California.

Kate McGonigal, Children unknown
Lucy, from the 1860 trip to England. Set up in New York at 110 West Thirty-Seven Street, but returned home when Isaac tried to sort his affairs out. I have never found a trace of her.

Ellen Brazee, who possibly bore him children.

Ellen Livingstone, who also possibly bore him children.

Mary Eastwood Walter, (known as Mrs Merritt) Lived at 225 West Twenty-Seven St, NY.
Children
Alice Eastwood Merritt
Alice Merritt was sometimes known as Alice Eastwood Walters and then Alice Singer. She married W A P La Grove in 1875, just before Isaac died. Alice used the stage name Agnes Leonard when pursuing her acting career in London.

Unfortunately the marriage to La Grove lasted just a few days, and later in 1885, she married the actor Frank Bangs. Their marriage lasted longer, almost a month!

2nd wife, Isabelle/Isabella Eugenie Boyer/Sommerville or Summerville.

Isaac was never sure how to spell her name so even in his will he made sure both spellings of Isabelle and Isabella were included.

Children

Adam Mortimer Singer

Adam Mortimer Singer KBE, (always called Mortimer or Morti to his close friends). Morti was born in America on 25th July 1863 and died 24th June 1929. As I mentioned much earlier, on Isaac's gravestone, where Adam Mortimer also lays, it states that Adam was Isaac's eldest son, which is clearly not the case. I guess they were having family problems even years later, and he thought he may have the last laugh.

He was certainly Isaac and Isabelle's first child and a great adventurer; he loved the open sky and wild sea. He became a balloonist, often trying to take photographs from high in the sky. Morti also became a pioneer aviator in Britain and France. Like his brothers he was an expert horseman and gave generously to the area of Paignton, especially the church and hospital.

Mortimer was also a keen yachtsman with his own yacht often moored in Paignton Bay. In 1920 he was awarded the KBE for converting much of his Berkshire home, Milton Hill, into a war hospital and convalescent home at the outbreak of The First

World War in 1914.

He became Governor of Guy's Hospital, Justice of the Peace and Sherriff of Berkshire.

Winnaretta Eugenie Singer (born in 1865 Yonkers, NY, died 1943).

Washington Merritt Grant Singer born 1866, died 1934. (Born aboard the SS City of Washington).

Paris Eugene Singer, born in Paris and sometimes spelt Eugenie. Born 20 Nov 1867, died 24 June 1932.

Isabelle Blanche (Belle) Singer 1869-1897, born in Paris, sometimes called Isabella, became Duchess de Cazes.

Franklin Morse Singer, born in Paris but left within the year. Born 12 Feb 1870, died 10 Aug 1939.

Chapter 57

There are so many offspring from Isaac, I have cherry-picked a few of the more interesting ones to see what they got up to. The picture below is Washington Singer in 'hunting pinks'. The horn and dress denote that he was Master of South Devon Fox

Washington Singer in his riding garb.

Hounds. Because of his generous donations, Washington Singer has a building named after him at Exeter University (opened by The Prince Of Wales in 1931).

Washington was also a racehorse owner and breeder, and steward of the Jockey Club. Along with Paris and Mortimer Singer, he invested heavily in Paignton and the surrounding area, building the Merritt Flats in Paignton and other dwellings. Washington did not have any children, though he did adopt two boys.

Winnaretta Eugenie Singer

Winnaretta Eugenie Singer held the prestigious title of Princesse Edmond de Polignac (1834-1901), wife of Edmond Melchior Jean Marie, Prince de Polignac. I am unsure why there is an extra 'e' on the end of Princess, but that is how it is spelt on her grave. 8 Jan 1865 – 26 Nov 1943.

She was by far the most interesting of Isaac's children and well worth a book in her own right. Winnaretta was known as 'Winnie' and was one of Isaac's favourites.

I read a lovely quote about Winnie by one of her husbands, but can't for the life of me remember where. It went something like, "I was infuriated by an American woman buying the Renoir, so I married her and had both."

Winnie adored her flamboyant father, and was only 10 when he died. She wrote in her diary every day, wondering how she would get through the long lonely day without her 'dear Papa'.

Princess of Polignac, Winnaretta Eugenie Singer.

She grew up with immense wealth and by all accounts, had a similar nature to her father. She loved to party and sought out excitement.

Winnie married her first prince in 1887. He was Prince Louis de Scey-Montbéliard. Things did not go well, and it is possible he was attracted more to her money than her personality. She later said that her marriage was never consummated, however that may have been an attempt to upset him. Anyway, legal proceedings were put into action and by 1891, she was free to marry the composer Edmond Melchior Jean Marie, Prince de Polignac, which she did in 1893.

Although she married two Princes, allegedly she also seduced half the wealthy women of Europe. Virginia Woolf apparently noted that to look at her, you could never guess that her real purpose was to seduce you. If you looked into her eyes you could easily get lost, she had a hypnotic and seductive look inherited from her dear Papa.

Winnie was flamboyant, pretty, rich and artistic, and was known for much of her life as the Princess of Polignac.

She was devoted to the arts, sponsoring great talent when she found it, with an endless list of beneficiaries who earned lifelong commissions to compose music. The list includes Debussy, Ravel, Stravinsky, DeFalla, Erik Satie and many, many more.

In 1888 she bought her house in Paris, which still survives today as the Singer-Polignac Foundation, handing out awards to scientists and musicians. Her true love seems to have been Violet Trefusis, who she became devoted to sometime after the First World War.

When she died, at around 78, she was one of the richest women in Europe and knew just about everyone of importance. Apparently she had a grand funeral with many of the great artists of the day in attendance.

Isabelle Blanche Singer
1869-1896

Isabelle Blanche Singer (Belle) became a Paris sensation, after moving with her mother and siblings back to Paris. She was the beauty of her age, marrying the Duke of Decazes, from one of the oldest and most respected French families.

The wedding was a spectacular affair with nobility attending from all around Europe. Thousands of well-wishers tried to get into the church to catch a glimpse of the young Belle in her wedding gown, which cost a king's ransom.

Belle had a daughter, Daisy Fellowes, but something went tragically wrong in her life, which I have yet to uncover. In 1896, at only 27 years old and in the prime of her life, she apparently took her own life.

Chapter 58

Paris Eugene Singer

Paris E Singer 20 Nov 1867 – 24 June 1932.

Paris Eugene Singer is just so fascinating that I have given him two chapters of his own.

Paris Singer helped run Oldway Mansion for many years and started an affair around 1908 (though it may have been earlier), with the famous dancer and actress, Isadora Duncan after falling hopelessly in love with her whilst watching her performances. This was scandalous news and the tabloids around the world loved every second, as the son was doing what his father had done.

Paris Singer was already married to the stunningly beautiful Cecilia, 'Lily' Graham, who he had met as a lad in Tasmania when he was on a world tour.

Lily was under age and a ward of the court, but Paris fell head over heels for her. Paris had to make a decision; he knew he would probably not get back to Lily, so instead they ran off to Europe together with his tutor (who was travelling with him). He married Lily, and in Paris they applied to the British courts to allow Lily into England. They were successful, and Lily came to live at Oldway. That must have been some day when she first set eyes on the amazing mansion after living in 19th century Tasmania.

For 20 years, Paris and Lily were fabulously happy and Lily bore Paris five children; Herbert, Cecil, Winnaretta, Paris and George, but unfortunately the blood of Isaac ran through Paris's veins and he had a wandering eye. By 1907 Lily and Paris agreed to separate, mainly because Lily was pretty sure that Paris had been carrying on with Isadora Duncan. Remember, Paris was fabulously wealthy, tall and athletic, and by all accounts amazingly handsome. Though separated, Lily stayed on at Oldway.

Cecilia, Lily Graham (sometimes spelt Lillie) had married Paris Singer around 1887. Stunning or what! They separated in 1907 and divorced in 1918, though Lily stayed in Paignton until her death on 7 March 1951. She was 84. Lily and Paris had five children.

Paris chased Isadora and eventually all his flowers and gifts paid off, for by 1910 Isadora Duncan and Paris were living in his London house.

He soon moved her to the West Country, where he could have her all to himself. In London she was a celebrity, and men followed her like bees around honey. In fact it was the way Paris himself had caught her, waiting behind the stage door after her performances.

I cannot imagine how Isadora got on living in the same house as Lilly. Isadora gave birth to their child, Patrick, while she was living there. It's lucky that the palace had so many rooms! Here Paris spoilt her, buying her everything that the heart could desire, even a yacht to look at in the bay. Staff pampering to her every whim surrounded her.

Paris Singer then bought a villa on the French Riviera, Villa Les Rochers, in Saint Jean Cap Ferrat. While he changed the architecture, a hobby he loved, he treated Isadora like a princess, even landing by seaplane in the bay, which their beautiful house overlooked. However, it still wasn't enough, and eventually Isadora left him. Apparently Paris even bought her Madison Square Garden but she threw it back in his face.

You see, unfortunately, Isadora was a struggling communist. Half of her wanted to suffer for her art, but she had the soul of a hedonist and adored the high life. She was constantly pulled between her feelings and her political ideals. It would be impossible for someone with such beliefs to marry Paris, a man who had everything.

Isadora also had a wandering eye and was particularly susceptible to pretty young things. Isadora was no beauty herself, but the long-limbed dancer oozed sexuality. She was also a superbly talented artist and had a hypnotic influence over men and women (which she used to full effect).

Unfortunately Isadora is like a tragic heroine from a

Shakespeare play; she rolled from one catastrophe to another. After leaving Paris Singer, the Californian dancer toured Europe with her children; a daughter, Deirdre Beatrice by Gordon Craig, a theatre designer and Patrick, the son of Paris Singer.

In the spring of 1913 her children were travelling with their nanny when the car narrowly avoided a collision near Boulevard Bourdon and stalled. The driver got out of the car to restart it by cranking handle but forgot to engage the handbrake, and the car was still in gear. The car suddenly jumped into life and lurched down the embankment, rolling into the River Seine. Both Patrick, who was three, and Deirdre who was seven, drowned along with the nanny.

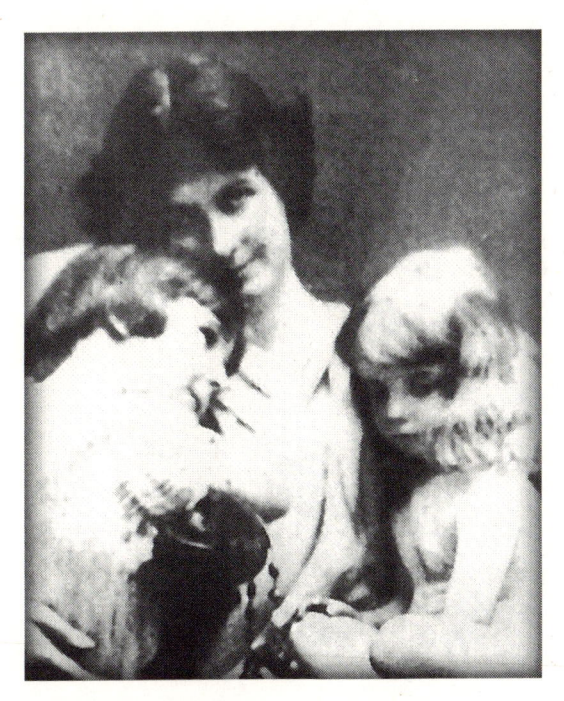

Isadora Duncan with Patrick and Deidre.

Heartbroken, Isadora was later convalescing when she also involved a car accident. She decided to leave Europe and went home to America. Originally she was forced to leave America because of her communist beliefs, but the restrictions were lifted and she opened her dance school there.

Although she could never marry the opulently wealthy Paris Singer, there was nothing to stop her marrying the poor Russian poet, Sergei Yesenin, who was 18 years younger than her. It was a short-lived romance, for he soon returned to his motherland. Some say Isadora chased him there, but was involved in yet another nasty car accident in Leningrad in 1924. In 1925 Yesenin, just 30 years old, committed suicide.

By the time Isadora was 50 her glory years were well behind her, and although still a communist she stayed in the best hotels, often telling the hotel to send the bill to Paris Singer. I never found out if he paid any of them!

Her drunken follies became famous until it all ended tragically on 14 September 1927. A gypsy had told Isadora many years before that she would never grow old and the curse came true. On a cool September evening on the French Riviera Isadora was leaving a party with Benoit Falchetto. Some say to have some fun, some say to learn how to drive. Her friend Mary Desto Perks (who was helping her complete her memoirs), had given her a hand painted silk shawl, which Isadora wrapped around her to keep her warm in the cool air.

The pair drove off in a two-seater open-top French Amilcar sports car, just after 9.30pm. Being an open car, somehow part of the shawl apparently got twisted around the wheel and axle. Just ten minutes after leaving Mary Desto, Isadora was ripped from the car by her scarf where she hit the pavement with such force it broke her neck.

The news made headlines around the globe and some small part of me thinks that the dramatic artist would have approved of her final 'spectacular and tragic' exit that so shocked 'her public'. Isadora had lived and died by one of her most famous sayings, "You were wild once. Don't let them tame you."

Although Paris Singer and Isadora had parted, he was devastated by her death and it tainted his old family home of Oldway for him, where he had many happy memories with her.

Chapter 59

Paris Singer & Palm Beach

Now we have to step back a little, returning to Oldway once more.

Paris Singer loved the finer things in life, big houses, fast cars and beautiful women. I have been told that the first ever order for a Rolls Royce motor car was placed personally to Henry Royce by Paris Singer. Funnily there is a road in Exeter called Paris Street, named after Paris Singer, not Paris France.

After the war and the loss of Isadora, Paris found that he now enjoyed life in other countries, especially America.

In failing health, he looked for a comfortable climate and found it in Florida, where he and Isadora had broken up (when Paris discovered her with the boxer Kid McCoy).

He was travelling with his pretty nurse, Joan Bates (also known as Joan Balsh and Anne Charlotte Bates), who had worked at Oldway when it was a military hospital and was looking after several of his Red Cross hospitals in Europe.

Oldway Hospital during World War One.

The two may have been having an affair for some time, but he finally divorced Lily and married Joan. After settling in Florida he took American citizenship.

Paris Singer had convinced himself that he was on his last legs and had settled in Florida to die a peaceful death. Ah, but things changed, A new wife, a new home and money to burn.

While in Florida he met a fellow sufferer who also thought that he was dying. He was the architect Addison Mizner. As they compared illnesses they formed a life-long friendship. Funnily enough, they both recovered.

Paris Singer then kept Mizner on a permanent retainer to develop Palm Beach. Addison was paid $6,000 a year to work exclusively for Paris and the Palm Beach area.

Singer founded much of what is Palm Beach today, investing heavily in Florida real estate. Who would guess that the great resort owes much of its development to the humble sewing machine!

He bought and started to develop a beautiful Island off the coast of Palm Beach, which he named Singer Island. He supposedly paid the enormous sum of $4,000,000 for the island, which sounds extortionate and hasn't been confirmed.

His idea was a bit like at home in Paignton, to build hotels and golf courses, but fate had other plans. A huge storm in 1928 put paid to his developments and then he lost much of his wealth in the 1929 stock market crash. This was prophetic as when he left Isadora, she placed a curse on him, saying one day he would lose his money so that he could feel the pain of poverty. This never came quite true, as even with the huge losses from the Wall Street Crash, Paris was always a wealthy man. However, the pressure of his failures did take their toll, for he became ill once more.

Paris Eugene Singer died back in London on 24 June 1932 and was buried next to his father. And so we leave the amazing Paris Singer to history.

Chapter 60

Now I think I may have this correct. Paris Singer named his only daughter Winnaretta. She went on to marry the eldest son of Baron Leeds, Commander Sir Reginald Arthur St John Leeds Bt RN, becoming Lady Leeds.

He was nine years her junior and died in 1970. She lived at Oldway and then Little Oldway, the smaller villa just behind the palace. It was the place her grandparents had lived in while Oldway was being built. She lived at Oldway until she died on 19 January 1980. Interestingly, Lady Leeds refused to see any visitors that claimed to be relations of Isaac Singer.

Shortly before she died, she insisted on being moved into the same bedroom in the villa that Isaac Singer had died in all those years previously. What an interesting request, and I wonder what was going through her mind in those last days of her life. Lady Leeds was the last connection with the Singer family and Oldway. The estate had been sold to Paignton Council just after the war in 1946 to avoid crippling death duties.

As I have mentioned, Paignton Council paid £46,000 for the estate, a huge sum, even with the buildings in poor repair. To put this into context, the average price of a house in 1946 was less then £500.

Chapter 61

Franklin Morse Singer
& Florence Singer

Franklin Morse Singer was born in February of 1870 and married Emilie. He seems to have been the more introverted member of the family (if that is possible), collecting antiques, racing his cars and breeding Arabian stallions, of which many European offspring are today descended. He died in Paris just after the outbreak of World War II in August of 1939.

Countess Von Dyhrn.

The Countess de (Von) Dyhrn was Florence Singer (born 1883 New York City), daughter of William A Singer, Isaac's first son. Although William had not been left a substantial amount on his father's death ($500), Isabelle had made sure he was well compensated and his mother (Catherine) had done amazingly well out of stalling Isaac's will.

Much of that money eventually went to William, and his daughter was brought up accordingly. When she was 22 years old she was sent to Paris to live with Winnaretta Singer, Princess de Polignac, and lived there with her cousin, Daisy, Princess Decazes de Glucksberg. They all lived at 43 Avenue Georges Mandel.

Florence became a devoted art lover and with her wealth supported artists just as Winnaretta had done.

Like the rest of her family, she moved in the best circles and was friends with some of the great names of the day, including Proust and Montesquiou.

While visiting her parents in America, Florence went to a party in Newport, laid on by Alva Vanderbilt who was a close friend of Sarah Webb, William Singer's wife. Sarah Webb's brother, William S Webb, was married to Eliza Vanderbilt.

The party at Newport in Rhode Island was a fabulous and glittering affair, and while there, Florence met and fell madly in love with a young count.

After a whirlwind romance she married the Count Franz Von

Dyhrn-Waldenburg (Baron Von Schonau) in 1913. He was a distant relative of Winston Churchill-Spencer and related to some of the most important European aristocracy.

While travelling in Egypt during the spring of 1914, Florence gave birth to a daughter, Desiree.

However, tragedy was to follow. Florence received word that her father William was seriously ill in New York and she made the decision to rush home. While on route, her daughter caught a chill that turned deadly and Desiree died. Heartbroken, Florence carried on to New York only to find her father also on his deathbed. He died shortly after.

Florence returned to Egypt and with her husband spent many years travelling between their properties in Germany, France, Egypt and America. Franz died in 1934 and a year later she moved to the centre of Konigsberg in Germany.

Tragedy struck once more when, during World War II, the British carried out a massive bombing raid on Konigsberg on 30 August 1944 and Florence Singer, Countess de Dyhrn was killed.

SINGER

Chapter 62

The Final Chapter

Did you ever think we would get here? In my final chapter I will wrap things up a little but before I start, can you imagine how many people are actually related to Isaac Singer today?

All in all, the Singer name became synonymous with wealth and power. Not bad for a little runaway. Now you see why I started this story by saying what a man!

While the family was growing, so was the Singer business. The Singer Company continued to grow and expand, building one of the first skyscrapers behind Isaac's old building in New York. Like his dream, it really did seem to touch the sky.

Factories were built in every major country in the world and Singer's dominated the sewing machine industry for over a century with its great products.

I have one final fact to finish our story. I mentioned earlier that the Singer factory in Britain had been built over the border in Kilbowie, Scotland, to avoid some of the English sewing machine patents that were still in force. The factory had its own docks, shipyard, railways, and even forests for wood. At its peak the factory employed around 14,000 workmen.

This is so brilliant – one of the problems the factory had was getting the men to work on time. Yes they had hooters and claxons but they did not work well over the din of the factory or the Scottish weather. In the 19th century very few working class people had a clock or watch, and thousands of workers turning up at roughly the right time was not a good way to run a precision business, so a solution had to be found.

It is hard to imagine the Kilbowie Factory
but to give you an idea here are some of its men.

The problem was solved by Singer's building the largest clock in the world, larger than Big Ben in London. Everyone in the valley could look out their windows and see the time. There was no excuse to ever be late again.

The huge clock tower survived right up until the 1980's.

The largest clock in the world on Singer's building.

And Finally a big Thank You

For the final few pages I was going to do the usual bibliography but that is so cold and goes nowhere near showing how much so many people have helped in putting this book together. I am sure that over the decades as I scribbled away I have missed out some important people. Please forgive me, it is not intentional, and do let me know. I will list anyone missing in the next edition (that's me being positive).

To begin, I must thank Graham Forsdyke and Maggie Snell, founder members of ISMACS, the International Sewing Machine and Collectors Society. Their inspiration has not only helped to build one of the finest societies in the world, but has also constantly inspired me. For their encouragement, dedication and enthusiasm over these many years I will always be thankful.

I must thank the countless people who have helped with the research in this piece from The Smithsonian, Victoria & Albert and Bodleian Library in Oxford, to the wonderful British Library with its amazing facilities and so many other museums.

Yolande Deveraux supplied some excellent information about Florence Singer and another relative, Jay Brewerton, added some fascinating pieces of family folklore.

There have been many complete strangers on the Internet who have seen Isaac's story and added snippets of their own information, as well as sending in pictures, which have added so much. Hardly a month went by without someone adding another piece of the puzzle.

All the extra information has all been so helpful during my years of research and I deeply appreciate the help from my old friends at ISMACS and everyone from Torquay/Paignton and Torbay Councils.

Thank you to the endless libraries, especially Torquay, Torbay and Paignton and to the patent offices. Also to West Dumbarton Council, who hold the finest collection of Singer sewing machines and have been so helpful.

A great thanks to the family members of the Singer dynasty, including the family of Charles Eastley and to the staff at Oldway who I pestered so often, as well as the Paignton, Torbay and Torquay hotels and museums.

Well my friends, decades of research, blood sweat and tears finally finishes here. It is my dearest hope that you have enjoyed this story as much as I have enjoyed researching and writing it.

BUT, it is not the end I have just opened the first door on an

TALES FROM THE COAST by Alex Askaroff
Large format paperback 384 pages, illustrated with dozens of pictures
ISBN 978 0-9539410-5-6 £14.99

Tales from the Coast continues the series of short true stories in which Alex Askaroff brings both England's history and her people vividly to life. Although they are local stories with Alex's easy writing style and humour they have had world-wide appeal. Alex's American publishers have launched his books in over 40 countries worldwide. and they were some of the first books on digital media like the Apple iPad and Kindle.

Alex Askaroff, a Sussex lad, left a thriving family business in specialty textiles to become a journeyman, travelling our county repairing sewing machines, carrying on a trade that he has known since a child.

This master craftsman has the enthusiasm of a poet and a pure love of story-telling. As Alex brings sewing machines back to life he also picks up local stories, history and gossip. And what stories they are!

The stories in **Tales from the Coast** are as pleasurable as a warm bath after a long hard day. All the stories are inspired by and related by the people who actually lived them. These are real people, no media sensations, just ordinary hard working people who, through their long lives, have had fascinating incidents indelibly burned into their memories.

Tales from the Coast celebrates the spirit of Sussex life, its people, colour and vibrancy. Dorothy tells of her years of hop picking even as the Battle of Britain rages overhead, Sheila tells of her encounter with a jaguar in the jungle far from home, Flo tells of her evacuation as a child and her glorious years on the farm far away from harm.

From the disappearance of Lord Lucan in Uckfield to the Buxted Witch, from William Duke of Normandy to Queen Elizabeth's Eastbourne dressmaker, **Tales from the Coast** is crammed with a fascinating mix of true stories that will have you entranced from start to finish.

amazing story. I am brought to mind of a short paragraph in one of Winston Churchill's great speeches. "Now, this is not the end. It is not even the beginning of the end. But it is, perhaps, the end of the beginning."

Alex I Askaroff

Sir Sewalot, fearless protector of the Sewalot Site.
Visit www.sewalot.com

And finally a big Thank You

For the final few pages I was going to do the usual bibliography but that is so cold and goes nowhere near showing how much so many people have helped in putting this book together. I am sure that over the decades as I scribbled away I have missed out some important people. Please forgive me, it is not intentional, and do let me know. I will list anyone missing in the next edition (that's me being positive).

To begin, I must thank Graham Forsdyke and Maggie Snell, founder members of ISMACS, the International Sewing Machine and Collectors Society. Their inspiration has not only helped to build one of the finest societies in the world, but has also constantly inspired me. For their encouragement, dedication and enthusiasm over these many years I will always be thankful.

I must thank the countless people who have helped with the research in this piece from The Smithsonian, Victoria & Albert and Bodleian Library in Oxford, to the wonderful British Library with its amazing facilities and so many other museums.

Yolande Deveraux supplied some excellent information about Florence Singer and another relative, Jay Brewerton, added some fascinating pieces of family folklore.

There have been many complete strangers on the Internet who have seen Isaac's story and added snippets of their own information, as well as sending in pictures, which have added so much. Hardly a month went by without someone adding another piece of the puzzle.

All the extra information has all been so helpful during my years of research and I deeply appreciate the help from my old friends at ISMACS and everyone from Torquay/Paignton and Torbay Councils.

Thank you to the endless libraries, especially Torquay, Torbay and Paignton and to the patent offices. Also to West Dumbarton Council, who hold the finest collection of Singer sewing machines and have been so helpful.

A great thanks to the family members of the Singer dynasty, including the family of Charles Eastley and to the staff at Oldway who I pestered so often, as well as the Paignton, Torbay and Torquay hotels and museums.

Well my friends, decades of research, blood sweat and tears finally finishes here. It is my dearest hope that you have enjoyed this story as much as I have enjoyed researching and writing it.

BUT, it is not the end I have just opened the first door on an

The latest book from the master story-teller
HAVE I GOT A STORY FOR YOU
Alex I. Askaroff
Country Books paperback 230 x 150mm
294pages £14.99 **Special price £12.50**
56 black and white photos
ISBN 978-1-906789-85-5

We all love stories, and in Alex Askaroff's eighth book he continues with his fascinating travels around the South East of England, collecting more hilarious and enchanting tales as he goes. Some will make you laugh, some will make you cry, but all will have you captivated.

Once again Alex brings his unique magic to the page and captures England, its history and its people, as only he can.

Includes 10 poems from the master's pen.

Alex I. Askaroff

TITLES BY THIS AUTHOR:

Crows Nest Publications (Random Thread Trilogy)
BK1 Patches Of Heaven   ISBN 0-9539410-4-3
BK2 Skylark Country   ISBN 0-9539410-2-7
BK3 High Streets & Hedgerows   ISBN 0-9539410-3-5

Tales From The Coast: ISBN 978 0-9539410-5-6
Norman, A Journey Through Time: ISBN 978-0-9539410-6-3

Fireship Press, Arizona:
Sussex Born And Bred: ISBN 978-1-935585-22-0
Corner Of The Kingdom: ISBN 978-1-61179-067-2

Country Books: UK
Have I Got A Story For You: ISBN 978-1-906789-85-5